The Little Bugler

The Little Bugler

THE TRUE STORY OF
A TWELVE-YEAR-OLD BOY
IN THE CIVIL WAR

BY
WILLIAM B. STYPLE

Belle Grove Publishing Company
Kearny, New Jersey
1998

Printed in the United States of America

Library of Congress Catalog Card Number 98-72201

ISBN 1-883926-11-4 (Hardcover)
ISBN 1-883926-12-2 (Paperback)

Belle Grove Publishing Co.
P.O. Box 483
Kearny, N.J. 07032

for Kimberlee

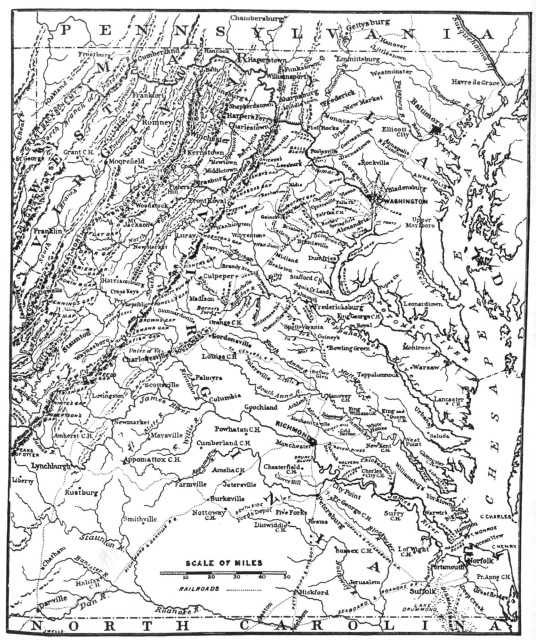

Map of Virginia in 1861.

Beat! beat! drums!—Blow! bugles! blow!
Through the Windows—through doors—burst like a force of ruthless men,
Into the solemn church, and scatter the congregation;
Into the school where the scholar is studying:
Leave not the bridegroom quiet—no happiness must he have now with his bride;
Nor the peaceful farmer any peace, plowing his field or gathering his grain;
So fierce you whirr and pound, you drums—so shrill you bugles blow.

Beat! beat! drums!—Blow! bugles! blow!
Make no parley—stop for no expostulation;
Mind not the timid—mind not the weeper or prayer;
Mind not the old man beseeching the young man;
Let not the child's voice be heard, nor the mother's entreaties;
Make even the trestles to shake the dead, where they lie awaiting the hearses,
So strong you thump, O terrible drums so loud you bugles blow.

Walt Whitman

BEATING THE LONG ROLL.

UNION CAVALRYMAN — THE WATER-CALL.

Introduction

Gustav Albert Schurmann was one of the youngest soldiers to serve in the Union Army during the Civil War. Considered a prodigy with the drum, little "Gus" was just past his twelfth birthday when he volunteered on June 26, 1861, to serve as a musician in the 40th New York Infantry. By the close of his distinguished military career at age fifteen, he had become a decorated veteran of ten battles and had served as bugler and orderly to four major-generals. Perhaps one of the most remarkable of all his experiences was the time spent as a guest in the Lincoln White House as the boyhood companion of Thomas "Tad" Lincoln.

Tad Lincoln has been called "one of the historic boys of America," and when this irrepressible spirit of fun and mischief first met Gus Schurmann, it was said that Tad "found his affinity." When one looks upon the photograph of the dashing little bugler taken in 1862, one may understand what Schurmann meant when he later wrote of how his friendship with ten-year-old Tad began:

> As I look back, I can see that I must have been an object of envy to "Tad," as by that time I had become quite a horseman, could blow a bugle, beat a drum, and swagger about like the bigger ones.

A war correspondent writing for the *New York Herald* was so impressed by the comradeship of the two boys that he asked prophetically in April, 1863: "Will their future histories be ever connected?" Unfortunately, historians have ignored the friendship of Gus and Tad, and their adventures together have long been forgotten.

Of all American wars, the Civil War is perhaps best known as the war fought by the teenage soldier. In fact, many who wore the blue or gray were mere children. Although the minimum age for enlistment without parental consent was officially eighteen years, young recruits often lied about their ages in their desperate efforts to enlist.

In an era when there was a moral consequence in telling an untruth, the boys could avoid lying by writing the numeral 18 on a slip of paper which they then placed inside their shoes. When the recruiting officer asked how old they were, they could say truthfully, "I am over 18."

In 1866, the U.S. Sanitary Commission conducted a study of more than one million (out of 2.5 million) Union soldiers' enlistment records. A total of 10,233 soldiers were below the age of eighteen—773 were fifteen, 330 were fourteen, and 127 were thirteen or younger, including 27 who were ten or under.

In all cases, the youngest of these soldiers were enrolled as musicians such as drummers, fifers, and buglers, who were different from military bandsmen. In June of 1862, there were approximately 28,000 musicians in the Union army, half of whom were in regimental bands, leaving some 14,000 drummers and fifers in the ranks.

The role of music and musicians was vital to the military during the Civil War. In camp, drummers, fifers, and buglers served to announce military calls and also played various patriotic and sentimental melodies. These musicians were expected to master all 148 calls and tunes described in the Union field-music text, *The Drummers and Fifers Guide*, by the first day of enlistment. On the battlefield, their drumrolls and bugle calls orchestrated tactical movements by sounding as many as 67 distinct calls to guide their comrades in action.

When not musically engaged, musicians often performed such gruesome duties as carrying the wounded from the battleline to the field hospitals. There they served as medical assistants during battlefield operations performed by the army surgeons.

In the decade following the Civil War, Gustav Schurmann settled down to family life in New York City. He became involved in several veterans' organizations such as the Grand Army of the Republic and the 40th New York Veteran Association in which he served as secretary.

Upon Schurmann's death, several New York newspapers printed lengthy obituaries detailing his Civil War experiences and his friendship with Tad Lincoln. Some of the headlines proclaimed:

—TAD LINCOLN'S PLAYMATE DEAD!
—BUGLED FOR GEN. KEARNY AT 12
—THE YOUNGEST VETERAN DEAD

These obituaries celebrated the child who rode side-by-side with so many revered Americans--Abraham Lincoln, Phil Kearny, and Dan Sickles. At the end of his life, Gustav Schurmann was recognized as a true American hero. Today, the bugle that he carried and the uniforms that he wore are treasured relics in the New York State Armory Museum in Albany.

Recreating the life and times of a twelve-year-old soldier during the Civil War presented some challenges for me. On the one hand, I wanted to write a completely factual book, footnoted and documented for the scholarly reader. On the other hand, I wanted to present an informative and enjoyable story for young readers who might ask: *What was life actually like for a twelve-year-old boy in the Civil War?*

Unfortunately, Gustav Schurmann did not keep a diary and it is impossible to know exactly what he experienced on each and every day. So, for this story, I consulted dozens of regimental histories and first-person accounts to enable me to better depict his typical daily routines and military experiences. All principal sources are referenced in the bibliography, and there is a glossary of 19th century military terms beginning on page 173.

Since my source material on Gustav was limited, I fictionalized some minor dialogue to portray his life more vividly. This dialogue is preceded by a dash and appears without quotation marks. All documented, historical dialogue appears within quotation marks. Every character in this story is real and every military scenario actually happened. No history was invented or manipulated.

In July of 1997, I visited the gravesite of Gustav Schurmann in Woodlawn Cemetery, the Bronx, New York. After visiting the cemetery office and determining the location of the grave, I proceeded to the plot area and began a search. I soon spotted a badly damaged government headstone mostly sunken beneath the surface. Barely visible on the stone was the name "G.A. Schurmann." Behind this marker was the larger Schurmann-family headstone, now covered with dead ivy and long neglected. As I cleaned the gravesite and placed a small American flag upon it, I decided that I wanted this book to serve as a tribute to Gustav Schurmann, the Little Bugler, and above all, as a remembrance to all of the children who served in the American Civil War, 1861-1865.

William B. Styple
Kearny, N.J.,
February 4, 1998

Three Federal drummers.

More than 100,000 New Yorkers jam Union Square on April 20th, 1861, for a giant "war rally" which featured Major Robert Anderson, commander of the garrison of Fort Sumter.

Chapter One

After the election of Abraham Lincoln as President of the United States in 1860, seven Southern states seceded from the Union. South Carolina, Mississippi, Florida, Alabama, Georgia, Louisiana, and Texas formed the Confederate States of America, electing Jefferson Davis as their first President.

On Friday, April 12, 1861, in Charleston Harbor, the Federal garrison at Fort Sumter was fired upon by the Confederates, and the fort was surrendered the following day. By Monday, April 15th, President Lincoln issued a proclamation calling for 75,000 volunteers to put down the rebellion and restore the Union. Then Virginia, Arkansas, Tennessee, and North Carolina seceded from the Union and joined the Confederacy. The United States was at war with itself.

War fever swept New York City. Thousands of New Yorkers, eager to join any regiment, swarmed the dozens of recruiting stations that were set up throughout the city. Here flags waved and bands played the "Star Spangled Banner," "Hail Columbia!" and other military airs. Recruiting officers and politicians made thrilling speeches to immense crowds that responded with cheers. "The Union must and shall be preserved!" was the cry. What in the world was a patriotic twelve-year-old boy supposed to do?

In the spring of 1861, little Gustav Schurmann was carrying a shoe-shine box and blacking boots at three cents a shine in City Hall Park on lower Broadway. He was described by a friend as a "blue-eyed, rosy-cheeked, tow-headed little boy," standing four-feet, seven-inches tall. Gus was born in the Province of

Westphalia, Prussia, on February 4, 1849. The following year, his mother and father fled revolutionary Europe and emigrated to the United States. They settled in New York City and soon after, two baby girls were born to the Schurmann family.

Now, caught up in the bustling patriotic throng and longing for soldierly adventure, little Gus wanted nothing more than to be a drummer boy in a regiment that was going south to fight the Rebels. Though he was already considered a prodigy with the drum, he was still a minor and needed his parents' permission to enter the army. One evening after supper, Gus asked his mother and father for permission to volunteer.

 —No! Not my baby, said Caroline Schurmann. And besides, what would the army do with a young boy like you?

 —I want to be a drummer boy, responded Gus. Father taught me...

 —Stop! You'll break my heart for sure if you do this, cried his mother.

As expected, Caroline would not even entertain the thought of her beloved boy in the army. Gus saw the tears in his mother's eyes and felt bad about making her cry, but that did not quell the "war fever" that was burning inside of him.

Making matters worse for Caroline Schurmann was the fact that her husband Frederick had just volunteered to serve for three years as a musician in the 40th New York Infantry. Frederick Schurmann perfectly understood his son's desire to enlist but did not encourage him. He knew full well the hardships of military life. The elder Schurmann was born in Prussia in 1828, and was a very talented musician who spent many leisure hours teaching his son to play a variety of instruments. Frederick was also extremely devoted to the cause of preserving the Union. Having seen the adverse effects of the division of his native land, he felt a strong need to prevent a similar event from occurring in his adopted country.

Without informing his mother or father, Gus began drumming for recruits in nearby Chatham Square. The regiment being raised there was the 42nd New York Infantry dubbed the "Tammany Regiment" in reference to the Democratic Tammany Hall political organization. The regiment was made up of mostly Irish street-toughs, and Gus did not feel welcomed. After a few days, some of the older drummer boys grew jealous of Gus's skill with the drum and began to bully him. A fist-fight ensued. Gus put up a brave defense against the bullies and even sent one or two of them packing; however, as he was outsized and outnumbered, Gus left the Tammanies--bruised in body, but not in spirit.

That night, Caroline saw the black eye and cut knuckles on Gus and questioned him about his scrapes. Gus said that he was just "playing" with some of the boys, and was anxious to go back outside for more play. The next morning, while several of the neighbor women were hanging their wash, Mrs. Schwarz said that while she was in Chatham Square the other day she saw Gus drumming with the soldier boys.

—Ah, the poor boys! said Mrs. Schwarz. They go off to the great war, away from their homes, their mothers, their wives, and their sweethearts, all to be killed in battle!

—No, not my Gustav! vowed Mrs. Schurmann as she stormed off to find her boy.

—Ah, the poor boys, continued Mrs. Schwarz to the other neighbor women. They will never any more come back. Ah, war is so wicked!

That evening after supper, Gus fairly got it. His mother and father talked, threatened, and pleaded with him long into the night but to no avail. Fearing that the boy would run away and find some regiment that would take him, Frederick finally convinced his wife that it would be best if little Gustav would accompany him into the 40th Regiment so he could then keep a watchful eye over the child. Caroline regretfully agreed. Frederick then looked at his boy, slowly lit his pipe, and sighed heavily.

—Gustav, my son, if you are certain that this is what you want to do, tomorrow we will go and see if the colonel will take you in.

Gus was elated and could think of nothing else for the rest of the night. His dream was coming true. He would at last be a drummer boy!

On the morning of June 26, 1861, Gus was up bright and early. He kissed his mother and baby sisters good-bye and then left with his father for the camp of the 40th New York Volunteers, which was stationed at Yonkers. As the ferryboat steamed up the Hudson River, Gus imagined himself marching and drumming with the regiment. He was thrilled and could hardly wait to get to the camp. The short trip seemed to take forever but he really did not mind; at last he was going to find some adventure and excitement in his young life!

After arriving at the camp and walking down the long rows of tents, Gus could barely contain his joy. Father and son together approached the large white canvas regimental headquarters tent. The tent flaps were raised and Gus could see the colonel sitting at a table working on what seemed to be some important papers. The colonel was a thirty-year-old, distinguished-looking, robust man with fiery eyes. Frederick asked the sergeant-major, stationed outside of the tent, for the favor of speaking with the colonel regarding a new recruit. The sergeant-major approached the colonel who nodded and motioned for them to come in.

Entering the tent, Frederick presented the eager young lad to the commanding officer, Colonel Edward Johns Riley.

—Well, so whom do we have here? the colonel inquired.

—My name is Gustav Schurmann, said the boy politely.

Pacing around the boy, and eyeing him from head to toe, the colonel slightly frowned and shook his head in disapproval. "No, you won't do; I couldn't think of it. You're too small and too young," he said abruptly.

Gus's heart sank. He wasn't even going to have a chance to prove himself. Having that unpleasant experience with the Tammany Regiment was bad enough, but now this rejection from the colonel of the 40th Regiment was too much. His dream of becoming a soldier was shattered, and as tears began to well in his eyes, Gus turned away and left the tent.

Frederick, seeing the hurt in his son, entreated:

—Please, Colonel, I mean no disrespect, but my son is a fine boy and won't give you any trouble. He is quite grown up for his age and he is a very good drummer.

—I'm certain that what you say is true, said the colonel, but what we really need is a drummer boy who can keep up with the regiment and not miss a beat. I just don't think that he'll be capable of handling this.

—If you could just hear him play, sir, the elder Schurmann pleaded. Gustav! he called.

The boy, head still lowered, reentered the tent.

Seeing the downcast lad and the hopeful father side by side made Colonel Riley reconsider his hasty rejection.

—All right, then, boy, take up that drum and beat.

Gus became enlivened. He would show the colonel that he was capable even if he was small and young. As he placed the strap over his head and lowered the drum into position, he was suddenly aware that several of the men outside the tent were watching and laughing. They were laughing at him because the drum was nearly as big as he was. Gus felt even more determined to prove himself and wanted to convince everyone that he was the drummer boy they needed. He gripped the sticks and with a deep breath began to play the "Long Roll."

Some soldiers, on hearing this call, hurriedly came out of their tents and fell into line, buttoning their jackets, and straightening their caps. The sergeant-major quickly rushed to order the awkward squad back to their tents before the entire camp turned out. Colonel Riley, seeing this, smiled at Gus.

—Very well, you will do.

Immediately, the boy radiated with pride. He thanked the colonel and assured him that he wouldn't let him down.

As father and son left the headquarters tent, Frederick smiled and placed his arm around his boy.

—Your poor mother will not be happy about this, but the war shall soon be over and I will bring her baby home safe and sound.

—But I am no longer a baby, Father! *I am a soldier!*

Colonel Edward Johns Riley

Frederick and Gustav were assigned to Company I, and spent the morning becoming familiarized with their new surroundings. Later that day, every man, one by one, was thoroughly examined by the medical officer who sharply questioned each of them:

—Teeth sound? Eyes good? Any diseases?

Pitiable was the case of the unfortunate man who because of bad hearing, defective eyesight, or some other physical ailment, was compelled to don his civilian clothes and take the next train home.

After having been thoroughly examined, the men were now to be administered the Oath of Allegiance. An army officer from West Point was in camp for this particular duty. The whole regiment was ordered into line.

Attention! commanded the officer.

—Hats off and raise your right hand! Repeat after me the following oath: "I, state your name..."

A low murmur of many names followed. Gus was sure he heard a few actually say, "I, state your name."

Gus held his right hand aloft while he recited the entire oath. It only took about a minute, but his chest swelled with pride when he finished with, "So help me God!"

A loud and mighty "Hurrah!" rose from the ranks, with hats tossed high in the air.

—That's it boys, we belong to Uncle Sam now! announced one soldier to his comrades.

Top photo: A typical Union regimental drum corps. Bottom photo: The regimental band of the 114th Pennsylvania Zouaves.

Chapter Two

The 40th New York Infantry was also called the Mozart Regiment, named after the Mozart Hall (rivals of Tammany Hall) faction of the Democratic party. Many people supposed that the name of the regiment had been adopted in honor of the celebrated musical composer, but it was at the solicitation of the "Mozart Hall Committee" that the regiment took the name "Mozart Regiment."

At this time, the regiment received four hundred recruits from the State of Massachusetts, companies B, G, H, and K, and two hundred men from Philadelphia, companies A and F. The volunteer quotas from those states had become full and so the recruits came to New York to offer their services. In fact, only four hundred men in the regiment were actually New Yorkers: companies C, D, E, and I.

As Gus walked through the immense camp looking at the men and boys of the various companies, he realized that he *was* the youngest and smallest soldier in the entire regiment of 1,024 men. Except for his father, these members were all strangers to Gus. Among the "Mozarters," as they called themselves, were clerks, farmers, students, railroad men, iron workers, lumbermen, and fishermen; just about every trade known to man was represented in the ranks.

At first the men in the different companies, as yet having no regimental life to bind them together as a unit, naturally regarded each other as foreigners rather than members of the same organization. Consequently, there was some rivalry among the companies, as well as continual friendly chaffing and lively banter, especially at the time of evening roll-call. The names of the men became a source of amusement. When the sergeant of Company I called the roll, the men of Company B would pick out all the outlandish-sounding surnames and make all manner of puns on them, only to be similarly repaid during their own roll-call.

On June 28th, the Union Defense Committee came down to issue uniforms to the regiment. Gus and his comrades were called out, formed into line and marched up to the quartermaster's department to draw their uniforms. There were so many men to be outfitted, and so little time in which to do it, that the uniforms were passed out almost regardless of the size and weight of the prospective wearer. Each man received a pair of pantaloons, a short dark blue jacket and cap trimmed with red piping, a heavy black overcoat also trimmed and lined with red flannel, a shirt, shoes, a heavy gray blanket, an india-rubber blanket, and underwear.

With clothes in arms, Gus and his comrades marched back to their tents and proceeded to get into their new uniforms. The sight of everyone getting dressed caused the men to erupt with laughter, for scarcely one man in ten was properly fitted. It seemed nearly all the short men had received long pantaloons, and the tall fellows had drawn the short ones; some caps sat perched high upon heads, while others came down over the wearers' ears. William H. Pratt was a great strapping six-footer who could not be well-suited. The largest shoe furnished was entirely too small for him. As the giant vainly tried his best to force his foot in, his comrades gathered about him laughing and teasing him unmercifully.

—Why, you would think that they only allowed boys into the army, Pratt complained. A man like me needs a man's shoe, not a baby's!

Gus laughed as the jokes continued until the soldiers made all their exchanges. Since Gus was a small boy, the smallest uniform had to be found and given to him. But how proud he was when he buttoned his coat and placed his cap upon his head; he was at last a soldier! He had overcome every obstacle he had encountered thus far in order to achieve this goal. But this was only the beginning. Hardships and sufferings for both the boy and the nation were yet to come.

The uniform jacket worn by Gustav Schurmann.

The Mozart Drum Corps was organized while the regiment was still in Yonkers, where all the military calls were learned and first performed. Each day there was reveille and roll-call at five o'clock in the morning, guard mount at nine, company drill from ten to twelve, dinner-call at noon, regimental drill from two to four, dress parade at five, supper-call at six, and tattoo-call (signaling "lights out") at nine. Throughout these long summer days the drummers and fifers continually practiced until their hands were sore and fingers blistered. It was not all fun and adventure after all. Although the lessons and practice wore Gus out, he took pleasure in the company of his comrades. He admired the musical talents of many of them and ambitiously sought to improve his own technique.

At this time, the drum corps was composed of twenty snare drummers (two for each company), six fifers, and a bass drummer. Charles T. Smith, a veteran of the Mexican War, was appointed Drum Major, and under his tutelage the corps soon became proficient. Andrew J. Mulkern was mustered in as Fife Major and few fifers could match his mastery of the instrument. The membership of the drum corps consisted of boys under the age of seventeen, all from good families.

Federal drummers.

Five of the ten companies of the Mozart Regiment had a bugler in the ranks to echo the calls of the regimental bugler, who stayed close to the colonel, ready to relay his orders instantly with piercing horn calls.

Though the drum corps had only a short time to practice together, they were highly praised. There were a good many singers amongst the members, and sometimes while marching to the drillfield, they would start up "John Brown's Body" or some other tune, which would be taken up by the whole regiment in one grand chorus.

> *John Brown's body lies a-moulderin' in the grave,*
> *John Brown's body lies a-moulderin' in the grave,*
> *John Brown's body lies a-moulderin' in the grave,*
> *While his soul goes marching on.*
>
> *We'll hang Jeff Davis from a sour apple tree,*
> *We'll hang Jeff Davis from a sour apple tree,*
> *We'll hang Jeff Davis from a sour apple tree,*
> *While his soul goes marching on.*

After one tedious morning of drilling, Gus and the boys of the drum corps played what the soldiers called "roast beef," or dinner-call, signifying their noon meal.

—Fall in for your hard-crackers! Gus heard the commissary sergeant shout.

With haversacks in hand, the hungry soldiers all ran towards a wagon drawn by two mules. Numerous wooden boxes marked with the letters "B.C." were unloaded while the men stood in line to receive their rations. The soldiers were each given ten pieces of rock-hard crackers called hardtack. These were plain flour-and-water biscuits, about four inches square.

—Are we supposed to eat these or hit the Rebs over the head with them? asked the company wag. What does "B.C."

stand for anyway? Does it mean they were manufactured "Before Christ?"

—Brigade Commissary! answered the sergeant indignantly.

—A hungry man could eat his ten and still be hungry, mourned Private Pratt.

—I bit into one the other day and hit something soft, said the company wag.

—What was it...a worm? asked Private Pratt, earnestly.

—No, *a ten-penny nail!*

A Federal officer holding a piece of hardtack.

On Friday, June 28th, the 40th New York held its first dress parade. The reviewing dignitaries were New York City's Mayor Wood and several members of the Union Defense Committee who came up to Yonkers. Many other visitors were present for the event, including a large number of ladies. Regimental line was formed fronting the camp and an exhibition in the manual of arms was given, followed by the drum corps playing a patriotic tune. After making a speech, the mayor presented the regiment with a beautiful silk national flag and a regimental flag made of blue silk fringed with gold.

As each day passed, Gus enjoyed the life of a soldier more and more. The Mozarters had now become his second family, and there was no other place that he wanted to be than with them. Gus revelled in the companionship of the older boys who regarded him as a younger brother, and the fathers who saw in him their sons. Though Gus frequently thought of home and his mother and sisters, he eagerly anticipated the order sending the 40th Regiment to Virginia to fight in the upcoming battle that was sure to whip the Rebels back into the Union.

The long-awaited order for the regiment to proceed to Washington finally arrived on the morning of July 4th, 1861. The 40th New York was to embark on a steamer bound for Elizabethport, New Jersey, and then board a train headed south. Long and sad farewells took place at the dock between the soldiers and their families. Gus watched as solemn-faced men embraced grief-stricken women and children. No one knew when they would meet again. Perhaps never. For some, it would be never.

Caroline Schurmann came to the dock with her daughters to bid her husband and son farewell. Many tears were shed by the heartbroken family members. The two little girls placed some sweets that had been tied up neatly in a handkerchief into Gus's hand, and embraced their beloved older brother. Gus became filled with sadness.

—Oh, my Frederick and Gustav! Caroline cried. You go away and leave us all alone. What will become of us?

—I trust in God to protect us all, said Frederick stoically, but with great tenderness in his voice. You must wait patiently for us to return.

—But for *how long?* asked Caroline.

—Not long, he replied as the two little girls clung to his legs affectionately. Frederick reached down and placed a calming hand on each daughter's shoulder for a brief moment.

—Don't worry, we shall be home soon. Be good little girls for your mother. We will write soon and often.

Final embraces were hurried by the order, *Fall in Company I!*

As the soldiers began to take their places in line, all eyes looked upon Gus, who had been standing apart, unable to speak.

—Gustav, said Caroline, come say good-bye to your Mamma.

Gus slowly obeyed, and his tearful mother squeezed him tightly. Then she looked at him, as if for the last time.

—My little Gustav is now a soldier, she said softly. How much you have grown. Please promise me you will keep warm and safe and come home to me soon.

—Don't worry Mamma, Gus replied with tears of his own. I will be all right. He then turned away and hurried to his place in line with his head bowed, wiping at his eyes with his coat-sleeves.

All farewells were finally ended with a long blast of a steam whistle and the cry of "all aboard!"

"Three cheers for the Mozart Regiment!" someone shouted, and the dock erupted with huzzahs.

The people cheered, the air was filled with farewells, and pandemonium reigned supreme.

As the steamer pulled away from the dock, the soldiers waved to their loved ones until they slowly disappeared from view. And thus it was, with a cheer and a shout, the Mozart Regiment started off for war.

While they gently steamed down the Hudson, Gus heard some of the soldiers complaining about their cumbersome loads, which weighed between forty and fifty pounds. Their burdens consisted of a musket, a cartridge box with forty rounds of ammunition, bayonet and scabbard, cap box, a rubber and a woolen blanket, canteen with water, mess equipment (tin cup, tin plate, knife, fork, and spoon), haversack with rations, and knapsack. The knapsack usually contained a spare shirt and underclothes, stationery, a diary, photographs, bible, toothbrush, soap, and a mending kit called a "housewife."

When some of the soldiers griped about their heavy loads, the company sergeant slowly turned to face them. Sergeant Terence Brady, a forty-year-old bull of a man and veteran of the War with Mexico, stood tall with all his equipment on and sneered at the raw recruits.

—Don't get downhearted, boys. We have only 1,087 more days to serve.

—What's that? asked the men in a chorus.

—I say we have but 1,087 more days to serve. Remember, we enlisted for three years. That is 1,095 days. We have been in for eight days. That leaves 1,087 yet to serve.

—Oh, but you know that we enlisted "for three years unless sooner discharged," and this war won't last three years, said one soldier.

—Don't calculate too much on that, smiled the sergeant. I believe it is going to take more than three years to settle this thing.

A company of infantry drills to the rhythmic beat of a drummer.

Chapter Three

The war was under way, and it was clear that the first battle between the two armies was imminent. The Federal army was positioned in the defenses surrounding Washington, with the Confederate army just twenty miles away at Manassas Junction.

The Mozart Regiment arrived in Washington, D.C., at nightfall on Saturday, July 6th. The train stopped in front of a barrack that was constructed to temporarily shelter the regiments upon their arrival in Washington. The vast room was floored with boards. As the Mozarters unrolled their blankets, they received for supper a stale piece of bread, a slice of salt pork, and a cup of cloudy water.

The next morning, the Mozarters marched to their new campground on a hill north of the city and erected their tents. The camp was dubbed "Camp Scott," in honor of General Winfield Scott. From the hill Gus could see the nation's capital outstretched before him: the Treasury Building, the Capitol with its yet unfinished dome, and the White House. The sights were all impressive to Gus, but he thought that Washington did not compare with New York City. All the while on the march through the capital, Gus heard the men eagerly speaking of meeting the Rebels in battle; they were lamenting the fact that the war might end before they would have the chance to fight.

On the morning of July 9th, the Mozart Regiment was drilling in an open field beside the 2nd Rhode Island Artillery Battery, when the lid of an ammunition chest struck the percussion fuse of an artillery shell, causing an explosion in one of the horse-drawn caissons. The men riding on top of the caisson were killed instantly and several others were horribly wounded. The men of Company I broke ranks and ran over to help. Sergeant Brady quickly sent for the surgeon.

Gus was sickened by the sight of the bloody and torn corpses. It was the first time he had ever seen a man killed, and the images of the horrible accident burned into his mind's eye. It was an incident that he never forgot. For the first time Gus realized that war was not all just "flags waving" and "drums playing," but men fighting and dying.

At Camp Scott, sickness became rampant amongst the Mozarters. An epidemic of malaria had developed and persistent coughing plainly indicated that the only enemy for now was disease.

Frederick was among those who became seriously ill with ague fever. Weakened and unable to drill or march in the hot sun, he was sent to the camp hospital tent. At the first opportunity, Gus visited his father.

—How are you feeling, Papa?

—A little better, said Frederick, who turned to gaze upon his beloved boy.

—Will you be able to drill with us again soon? Gus asked, eager and hopeful.

Sensing his son's concern, Frederick smiled and said reassuringly:

—Don't you worry, Gustav, I'll be better in no time.

Gus rose to leave, then paused for a moment. He had never seen his father so sick before. It seemed not too long ago that the scene had been reversed, when his father and mother had cared for him during his childhood illnesses. He had never been in this situation before, and it made him uncomfortable.

As he lifted the tent flap, Gus heard a muffled cough and hesitated before moving on. He decided that he would wait before writing his mother about this; it was, after all, just a slight fever. It would pass.

Each day since arriving in Washington, the regiment expected marching orders to proceed to Virginia. The orders finally arrived on Friday, July 19th, directing the men to break camp the following day.

At four o'clock in the morning the soldiers were astir packing knapsacks, rolling overcoats and blankets, filling canteens and haversacks. They ate breakfast quickly, and at six o'clock assembled into line with all accoutrements on. It made no difference that the loads were heavy; the Mozart Regiment was ordered to Virginia and the men were happy to belong to the invading army. Though still ill, Frederick rallied from his sickbed to accompany the regiment on its first campaign.

Gus and the drum corps took their place at the head of the column and began playing a patriotic tune. "Forward to Richmond!" the men shouted, and with light hearts and quick steps the regiment started off, anxious to finally meet the enemy in battle. As the 40th New York Regiment marched down Pennsylvania Avenue, thousands of spectators cheered and ladies waved their handkerchiefs along the way. The soldiers marched to the wharf on the Potomac River and onto a steamer that carried them to the city of Alexandria, Virginia, a few miles downriver.

Upon arriving at the deserted city, Gus and his comrades disembarked and marched past the Marshall House, where Colonel Elmer Ellsworth had been killed the previous May while removing a Rebel flag from the rooftop. At noon they camped upon the ground vacated by the 5th Pennsylvania Regiment which had already advanced toward Manassas. The Mozarters had only to pitch their tents where the tents of their predecessors had stood. The camp was called Camp McDowell in honor of General Irvin McDowell, who commanded the invading army.

The Mozarters were not destined to occupy this ground for long. The following day, they were ordered to advance toward Manassas. Gus was concerned that his father might not be able to continue. The march into Virginia seemed to weaken Frederick further, but the elder Schurmann was determined to keep his place in the ranks and do his duty. His fever had returned, but the excitement of the impending battle made it tolerable. Whether or not he would be able to fight was questionable, however.

—How are you feeling today, Papa? Are you well enough to march? Have you heard where we are going?

—I feel much better, son. I wouldn't miss this battle for the world. There is a rumor that our army will attack the Rebels at Manassas Junction, not far from a creek called Bull Run, and if there is going to be a fight, I want to be in it.

The morning of July 21, 1861, was atrociously hot and humid; not a breath of air was stirring. The atmosphere was torrid and the men were stiff, sore, and filled with pains and aches from the march. By two o'clock in the afternoon, Gus and the other Mozarters were ordered to proceed to the Orange and Alexandria railroad station where a train bound for Manassas Junction awaited them. As the 40th New York embarked upon the train, they could hear the distant boom of artillery at Manassas, and each man quietly pondered his fate in the battle not far ahead.

On board the train, the officers made necessary preparations for meeting the enemy and ordered the men to load their muskets. After fifteen miles, the train halted at Fairfax Court House where the men disembarked to guard the railroad and telegraph lines; two men were left at each post about forty-five feet apart, with the line extending about five miles. The dull thud of artillery could still be heard in the distance.

The drum corps was stationed near regimental headquarters, located in an old farmhouse. From here, Gus surveyed the campsite and he believed they were very comfortably situated for their first campaign bivouac. At sunset, the men began to build small fires for boiling coffee and reached into their haversacks for a supper of bread and beef. Word had reached camp from the sentries along the railroad that the battle had ended just before sundown, and the anxiety subsided. There seemed nothing to fear. Gus was certain that the Union Army had won an easy victory. This presumption remained until an hour before daybreak when retreating Federal troops informed the Mozarters that the Union army had been badly beaten and stampeded at Bull Run.

For the next several hours, Gus watched as thousands of defeated men in blue passed by, some wounded, and many demoralized. The retreating soldiers complained that they had been poorly led and greatly outnumbered, and most were anxious for another fight on more equal terms.

Later that day, while the Mozart Regiment was acting as rear guard for the defeated army retreating towards Alexandria, Sergeant Brady approached Gus with the unfortunate news that Frederick had collapsed and the surgeon had sent him to the hospital in Georgetown. Gus was stunned.

—Is he all right? Can I go see him?

—He will be fine, said Brady. He should receive much better treatment in the hospital than in camp. Don't worry. We shall both go and see him when we return to Alexandria.

After the defeat at Bull Run, Major-General George McClellan was placed in command of the Union army and he quickly began its reorganization. Morale was soon restored and "Forward to Richmond!" became the cry once more. The Mozarters were particularly anxious for another chance to meet the enemy in battle as they were stung by criticism from other regiments who said that "the 40th New York did not smell the battle's smoke."

One of Gus's comrades in Company I sent a letter to the *New York Sunday Mercury* about the army's reorganization and the continued patriotic spirit in the Mozart Regiment:

We have had no excitement here for some three or four days past. A circumstance quite unusual. Troops are pouring into Washington by thousands, and no doubt, our long and grand forward movement will be made. Let us hope that our officers have learned a serious and instructive lesson within the past few weeks, and that when again we march, that it may be to victory. Have we not patriots enough--men who will fight till their last drop is spilt, who would sooner lose their lives than to see a single star blotted from our glorious flag? We have. Thank God, we have.

The Mozarters were encamped on the main road to Fairfax only a short distance from the city of Alexandria. New tents for the regiment were received from the quartermaster. They were the bell-shaped Sibley tent, styled after the Indian tepee, and had a ventilator on top. These tents accommodated fifteen to twenty men and kept Gus and his comrades reasonably comfortable during the summer weather in Virginia.

The first night in the Sibley tent was an adventure. At bedtime the boys filled the tent with catcalls, shouts, yells, snatches of song, and kept up a general hullabaloo till well after midnight. Then the snoring began--double bass, tenor, and baritone. In fact, there were so many types and variations that Gus found it hard to fall asleep. But sleep finally came, and it was a good sound sleep.

A few minutes before dawn, the sergeant-major stuck his head inside the tent.

—Up boys! Time for reveille!

The drummers rubbed their half-open eyes. They stretched, yawned, and kicked off their blankets, grunting and groaning from the stiffness caused by the hard bed and damp earth. As they reached for shoes, caps, and coats, another loud commotion commenced which spilled out into the company street. Immediately thereafter, the pounding of twenty drums awakened the camp and announced the beginning of another day.

Top photo: Officers, non-commissioned officers, and a drummer of Company I, 38th N. Y. Infantry pose in front of their Sibley tents. Bottom photo: Colonel Riley and the officers of the 40th N. Y. stand in front of the regiment in 1861.

During the long, seemingly endless summer days, Gus and the other boys in the drum corps had more time for mischief. Luckily, Colonel Riley had a rare sense of humor, and on many occasions petty offenders brought before him secured their release unpunished owing to their ready wit. One drummer was accused by a farmer of stealing a sheep and was brought before the colonel for judgment. When asked for an explanation, the accused soldier remarked:

—You see, Colonel, while out chopping firewood, this lamb which was in an adjoining field attacked me and in self-defense I killed it. I would kill this sheep or any other man's sheep that climbed over a fence and tried to bite me.

With a significant grin the colonel dismissed the case, but there was a suspicious smell of roast lamb pervading the camp that evening.

Although the regiment was officially known as the 40th New York Infantry, they retained the name "Mozart Regiment" all through the war. In fact, after the first few months, they were better known by that name in the army than by any other, except maybe that of "The Forty Thieves." This title was given to them by other regiments, which credited the Mozarters with greater foraging ability than they themselves could claim. When food was scarce and other groups of foragers returned empty-handed, the "Forty Thieves" succeeded in finding delicious plunder. Chickens, pigs, sheep, turkeys, and beef that had escaped the search of earlier seekers became easy prey for the Mozarters.

In addition to drilling at least four times a day, the Mozart Regiment was engaged in building Fort Ward and Fort Lyon. Soon the District of Columbia would be protected by a string of forts. The Rebels were fortified at Centreville about ten miles away and were an imminent threat, so the Mozarters had to remain on constant guard. While the men were busy building these forts, Gus and the drum corps spent most of their time practicing and, in the evenings, occasionally performing a musical concert.

Throughout the month of October, the 40th New York had easy duty picketing along the Potomac River. The weather was pleasantly warm and dry and the men were in good spirits. The golden days of autumn in Virginia agreed with them, and when not busy drilling, many of the soldiers in Company I engaged in informal games of baseball, playing both inter-company matches, and against the other regiments in the brigade. Corporal John Brown and several other members of Company I had been professional ballplayers before the war and were well-known to all New Yorkers and Brooklynites who were fans of the game. Brown had been the President of the Atlantic Ball Club and was perhaps the best ballplayer that Gus had ever seen. The corporal befriended Gus and even gave him a few pointers about how to improve his batting.

The following article, written by a member of Company I 40th N.Y., appeared in the Sunday Mercury, *September 8, 1861:*

BASE BALL IN VIRGINIA—THE MOZART REG-IMENT—The following letter from our special correspondent in the Mozart Regiment contains matter of general interest to ball players, and we therefore give it a place in this department :

FLAG HILL, NEAR ALEXANDRIA, VA., }
Tuesday, Aug. 20th, 1861. }

To the Editors of the Sunday Mercury :

Lest our friends should presume that our thoughts are upon war, and war only, I give below the result of a well contested ball-match, which came off some week or so ago. Among the number I have no doubt some of our Brooklyn friends will recognize old players, who more than once have gained the applause of enthusiastic hundreds. The following is the score :

FIRST.	O.R.	SECOND.	O.R.
Bennet (P.)	2 4	Brown (C.)	2 4
Lowery (C.)	3 4	Garrison (1st b.)	2 4
Wood (1st b.)	3 4	Ward (P.)	2 4
Torrens (2d b.)	3 3	Shute (c. f.)	3 2
Short (3d b.)	4 3	Leahy (3d b.)	4 3
Airy (c. f.)	3 3	Godfrey (r. f.)	4 2
Raynor (r. f.)	4 2	Burnton (s. s.)	3 2
Decker (s. s.)	3 2	Millen (2d b.)	4 1
Munson (l. f.)	4 3	Triqulet (l. f.)	3 3

INNINGS	1	2	3	4	5	6	7	8	9	
First	2	3	3	0	2	1	4	6	7	28
Second	2	5	0	3	3	4	2	0	7	26

Scorers—Samuel Valentine and James Willis. Umpire—Sergt. Richard Brush, of the Atlantic Club (of Jamaica, L. I.).

As you perceive, the game was a close one, and ended as creditable to the one as to the other. Among the "Firsts" there were some good players. Corporal Bennet made some splendid batting, and proved himself a good pitcher also ; he was a member of the Atlantic (of Jamaica). Lowery done well, and there is none who can excel him in catching ; he formerly belonged to the Mattano (of Brooklyn). Wood and Short were both excellent players, and are old hands at it. On the other side we noticed Corporal Brown especially. His batting was excellent, and generally gained for him a home run. Ward and Garrison played well also. Ward pitched with admirable swiftness, and gave that peculiar "twist" which won for Creighton so much praise. Altogether it passed off well, and was applauded by all who witnessed it.

Another match may come off soon, when the whole eighteen will be joined. The ball, however, will be that made by "Minie"—a little harder, I believe, than those usually used. I sincerely trust that we may be as successful in the new game as in the old.

Well, I know not whether I have penned an interesting letter or not, but still I trust that the reader will imagine the author to be knee deep in the mud, and almost wet to the skin ; then consider whether this is not as much as could be expected, when everything so teems with inspiration.

All are well, and in good spirits.

Yours, &c., FOAMUS,
Co. I, Mozart Regiment.

While Gus had some moments of enjoyment, he continued to worry about the health of his father. In his letters home, Gus never alluded to just how sick his father was. Disease had by now so weakened Frederick's condition that he became unable to perform any duty. Gus visited his father at the hospital as often as possible. During these visits, Frederick's spirit seemed to brighten and he passed the time teaching Gustav several bugle calls. Frederick stuffed an old rag inside the bell of the horn to muffle the notes while Gus practiced. Frederick would hum the notes and Gus would respond with the call.

One day, when their visit drew to a close, Frederick told Gustav to keep the bugle, as he would have no further use for it. Frederick had been told by the surgeons that he would be discharged from the army and sent home to recover.

Gus was dismayed, and suddenly became frightened of being separated from his father. Also there was the possibility that he could be discharged as a minor and sent home too. The boy fretted over this problem for several days.

Shortly before Frederick's discharge, Sergeant Brady, Corporal Brown and some of the boys in the drum corps accompanied Gus on a visit to the hospital to see Frederick. Sergeant Brady expressed his regret to the elder Schurmann about his condition, and reassuringly stated that if Gustav wanted to remain with the regiment his comrades would watch out for him.

—We will take care of little Gustav, never you fear for that. And as soon as Colonel Riley hears little Gus with your bugle, he will certainly know he has a first-rate musician.

—Besides being the best drummer in the regiment, added Corporal Brown, Gus is also the best short-stop in the drum corps!

—Thank you all for your kindness, said Frederick. Please, I would like to speak to Gustav alone for a moment.

As Brady, Brown and the rest of the soldiers rose to leave, Gus knelt beside his father's cot.

Looking at his beloved son, Frederick smiled weakly.

—Gustav, you must never forget why we enlisted to fight in this war. Our cause is just. We have taken up the sword for the purpose of defending and preserving our adopted country from a band of Rebels whose aim it is to destroy the best and noblest nation on earth. There is no doubt that this war is a terrible thing and many lives will be lost, and during the dark hours there will be times when your courage and faith will be tested. You can be sure, my son, that if you do your duty, your whole duty, courageously, you will serve your regiment and country well. So, if it is your wish to remain in the army and do your duty, you have my blessing.

Gus felt strengthened by his father's patriotism and stirring words. The boy's courage and devotion to the preservation of the Union was now unwavering.

—Yes, Papa, I want to remain a Mozarter and do my whole duty.

On November 15th, Frederick Schurmann received his discharge from the army. Gus received permission to accompany his father to the train station in Washington. Not many words were spoken between father and son. Each feared that this would be their last moment together, forever. While waiting to board the train, Frederick dropped to his knee and embraced his beloved boy.

—Put your faith in God, said Frederick, and He will bring you safely home.

—Yes, Papa, said a tearful Gus, unable to say more.

The whistle blew and Frederick feebly boarded the train. As the car door closed, father and son waved to each other until the train passed out of the station and into the darkness.

President Abraham Lincoln

Chapter Four

A Grand Review of General McClellan's newly reorganized Federal Army of the Potomac was to be held for President Abraham Lincoln, at Bailey's Cross Roads, Va. Many thousands of citizens and officials came from Washington to witness the imposing sight. To see a grand review of well-drilled troops was one of the finest and most inspiring sights anyone of the day could behold.

On Wednesday, November 20th, Gus and the drum corps were up before the sun. Since the distance from camp to the reviewing field was ten miles, the Mozart Regiment ate breakfast that morning at four o'clock, and commenced marching at sunrise, reaching their allotted position by ten o'clock. When General McClellan, President Lincoln, and their staffs appeared on the field, a thundering salute was fired by the artillery. As the reviewing officers passed on horseback, each regiment presented arms and the bands played.

Gus had never seen so many soldiers before. The review was comprised of about 80,000 infantry, 8,000 cavalry and 17 batteries of artillery. The boy felt proud to be part of the display and was glad to participate, but he was also disappointed that Frederick wasn't there to witness such an impressive sight. When the President came into view, the soldiers all tried to get a good look at him. Gus had heard so much about Abraham Lincoln in the past year; he heard him praised and condemned in equal measure. What struck Gus most was Lincoln's care-worn, gentle expression of sadness. He hadn't pictured the President that way at all. Gus was thrilled to see him in the flesh, and played his drum with all of his might as the Commander-in-Chief rode past. President Lincoln slowed his horse and lifted his stovepipe hat as a salute and the men cheered heartily. After the review, on the march back to camp, the boys in the drum corps were highly complimented by Colonel Riley.

By early December, the 40th New York completed building their winter quarters. Gus and his comrades made themselves as dry and comfortable as possible by placing boards on the ground inside their tents and using a small stove for warmth.

For two days each week, the regiment went out on picket duty, where they got little sleep and suffered much from the cold. When they were not on picket, all the men not needed for camp guard had to drill: regimental drill, brigade drill, and even division drill. Many an evening the tired men came in feeling more dead than alive.

One evening as Colonel Riley walked through the camp he paid a visit to Company I. Gus was sitting on a camp stool in front of a large warm fire with his comrades who were smoking their pipes and telling stories.

—I'm sorry that your father is so ill, Gustav, said Colonel Riley, but you know he will get better care now that he is at home with your mother.

Gus nodded, unable to speak. He never thought it would be this way, that he and his father would be apart. He knew that his mother would now want him to come home too and forget about the army. Was the colonel here now to send him home? Gus unconsciously held his breath for a moment.

—I heard you playing the bugle the other day, continued the colonel.

Gus was mortified. During his spare moments away from the drum corps, he had been practicing with his father's bugle, not wanting to forget what Frederick had taught him.

—I was very impressed. You are quite talented, just like your father, said the colonel. Perhaps you will be regimental bugler one day.

Gus returned a sheepish grin, quite relieved that he was not going to be discharged and sent home.

—That would be a great honor, sir, said Gus, looking up at the commanding officer with gratitude.

—I think that would make your father very proud, said Colonel Riley, who then continued with his walk.

During the winter months, Gus spent his spare hours practicing bugle calls. He was determined to be the best in the regiment and to prove to himself that he could master the instrument and play as well as his father. Because of his relentless drive and natural ability, it was not long before Gus became proficient. He earned the respect of his comrades, who regarded him with both admiration and mild amusement; for as small as he was, Gus was tough and spirited. He became very popular for not only being the youngest soldier in the regiment, but one of the most willing to perform any duty. And with Frederick no longer in the regiment, many of Gus's comrades sought to cheer him.

A seventeen-year-old Irish lad named Thomas Connolly was the other musician in Company I. It took only a short while for Gus and Tommy to become good friends, known in the army as partners or "pards." Nearly every soldier in the army had his pard. Pards usually divided the numerous little domestic duties like pooling their rations, taking turns at cooking, getting water, and altogether making themselves more comfortable and happy.

The members of Company I seemed to have more than their share of fun and jokes. In camp, on the march, and during the solemn hour of battle, there was always a laugh passing down the line or some sport going on amongst the men. Gilbert Abrams was the comic wit of the company, and a fair and honest man. He continually kept Gus amused with his unique storytelling ability and comical songs. Abrams liked to tell the boys tales about the Gold Rush and his mining days in California. He could spin an adventurous yarn that kept them all in good humor and chased away the homesickness. Every night, gathered by the campfire, the soldiers would call on Abrams for a story or a song. One of the favorite songs that Company I sang was printed in the *New York Sunday Mercury*:

> *Then hurrah for the camp, the lively camp,*
> *Where we watch through the night for alarms.*
> *Where the roll of the drum and the steady tramp*
> *Is heard at the order 'To arms.'*
> *Where each eve we meet old tales to repeat*
> *Of homes and firesides bright;*
> *And happy we grow as each picture comes slow*
> *From memory's hails of light.*

The enlisted men continually had fun joking and teasing one another, and many Mozarters were christened with odd nicknames. One hapless soldier with uncommonly bad luck was called "Jonah." Another particularly stout fellow who was talented with an axe was nicknamed "Mule." Drummer Willard Howe was one of the Massachusetts boys and wore spectacles. Without them he couldn't see a barn door ten feet distant. The drum corps chaps teasingly nicknamed him "Glass-Put-In." He always kept a supply of books in his knapsack, and many nights he would read aloud to his comrades. As a student during the early days of the war, Willard had been on his way to school the very morning that Company G was leaving for New York. With no idea of going along, but seeing some friends and acquaintances in line, he suddenly became stricken with a case of "war fever." He immediately ran across the street to a blacksmith's shop, crammed his schoolbooks through a broken window, took his place in line, and marched off with the boys without so much as saying good-bye to the folks at home.

As 1861 drew to a close, Colonel Riley began to notice and admire Gus's leadership qualities. Gus sometimes served as an orderly to the colonel and on a few occasions was designated as regimental bugler. But this coveted position did not excuse him from his duties as drummer for Company I. In fact, this meant he was given even more duties to perform.

As regimental bugler, Gus was the first man awakened in the morning, usually by the sergeant-major or adjutant. At about five o'clock in the morning, the camp was all quiet and a perfect stillness reigned. No one stirred, except a solitary sentry pacing up and down his lonely beat. The first sounds were made, perhaps, by the corps bugler, some distance away. Soon the division bugler answered, followed by the brigade bugler. Then, if there was a regimental bugler, he responded. The drum corps soon followed, and in a short time the sleeping camp was at once transformed into a bustling scene. Every soldier was busy doing something: some washing, others airing their blankets, while others were making fires to prepare breakfast. Every soldier was in a hurry, as other bugle calls were soon expected announcing other duties.

Bugle calls were, in fact, words of command, and some calls were pleasing, even musical, suggestive of what duties they were intended to indicate. After reveille, Gus played roll-call, then the "doctor's call," or, as the boys called it, the "quinine call." All ailing or indisposed were expected to answer this by reporting promptly to the doctor's tent for treatment. Guard-mount and then drill-call followed; in fact, there were calls for every line of duty.

Tattoo-call pleased Gus, for like reveille it was played by all the buglers as the order to retire. It signified that the soldiers' duty for the day was over; that they were to engage in preparing their beds for the night. After a short while there was another call, positively the last of the day. This was known as "retreat," or "lights out." Soon Gus was able to perform all the calls with perfect execution and was considered by all who heard him a much-accomplished bugler.

On Christmas Eve, Colonel Riley suggested that the men decorate the camp, and during the day the Mozarters obtained hundreds of cedar and fir trees, which grew in abundance. Each company street was adorned with them, and the flagpole was decorated with evergreens at the base.

The following day the soldiers had a holiday exemption from their usual duties. Christmas menu consisted of soup, beef steak, potatoes, fresh bread, and boiled rice. Thoughtful friends and families had sent boxes from home filled with many delicacies which were shared by all. After a concert by the drum corps, the boys were all treated to delicious mince pies. Despite the good cheer, Gus felt that the absence of his family lent a tinge of sadness to the merrymaking. In fact, all the Mozarters felt an intense yearning for home and loved ones, at this--their first Christmas in camp.

In January, 1862, when the doldrums of winter had set in, some of the officers had obtained leaves of absence for short terms, and homesickness spread like a fever amongst the Mozarters. Now it seemed that every man sought to obtain a furlough. Colonel Riley was besieged day and night with applicants until he was concerned, if not irritated. In a few instances furloughs for ten days were granted, which only made the others more desperate and urgent. Almost every conceivable reason or excuse was given for requesting a leave of absence, and in many cases conditions at home were misrepresented to obtain the coveted permission to return there. The colonel was generally able to detect deception, but in one case he heard a soldier's pitiful tale about his sick wife. The colonel told him he would consider the request and inform him in a few days. When three days had passed, the soldier again appeared at the colonel's tent with "sad news from home," saying that he must go at once if he desired to see his wife alive. Believing that the man was lying, Colonel Riley decided to test him, and the following conversation ensued:

"Your wife is very sick, is she?"

"Yes, Colonel."

"You have a letter saying she is sick?"

"Yes, Colonel."

"Well I have a letter from your wife also. She says she is well and does not want you to come home."

The private smiled and said, "Did you write a letter to my wife, Colonel?"

"Yes, I did."

"Did my wife respond to your letter, Colonel?"

"Yes, she did, and what do you mean by coming to me with a lie about your 'sick wife'? What have you to say for yourself?"

"Colonel, all I have to say is that we are two of the biggest liars in the Mozart Regiment."

"Why, Private, how is that?"

"Well, Colonel, I'm not married at all."

Though he had a unique sense of humor, Colonel Riley was a strict disciplinarian. When a soldier committed a military offense it was usually met with severe retribution. If a man refused to do his duty, he was at once hauled into the guardhouse. There the punishment varied at the discretion of the officers. Perhaps the offender was simply confined and put on bread and water, or maybe ordered to carry a log of wood or a knapsack full of stones.

The use of liquor by the enlisted men, either in or out of camp, was strictly prohibited. Somehow a soldier smuggled a bottle into camp and subsequently failed to control his appetite. Before he was even aware of it, the soldier had lost control of his senses. When his drunkenness was discovered, he was taken to the guardhouse and was tried by court martial the next day. He was found guilty of intoxication and sentenced to carry his knapsack filled with rocks on his back for two hours while marching around the camp, hands tied behind his back. Gus watched the guilty soldier for the entire two hours. He pitied the man, for the loaded knapsack must have weighed at least fifty pounds. The drunken soldier never indulged to excess again and the punishment had a restraining influence upon the others.

Later that winter, the Mozarters witnessed the execution of a deserter. One dark night, a private in another regiment approached a Federal picket post which he had mistakenly thought was a Rebel post, and informed them of his wish to desert to the enemy. The deserter was arrested, tried, convicted, and sentenced to death by firing squad. At the appointed hour, the entire division marched out and took position in a large field surrounded on all sides by pine woods. The division was drawn up to occupy three sides of a great hollow square. The fourth side of the square, with a recently dug grave, was left open for the execution. Scarcely were all the soldiers in position when they first heard the mournful notes of the "Dead March." Looking away in the direction whence the music came, Gus watched as a long procession marched slowly to the measured stroke of a muffled drum.

First came the band playing the dirge, next the squad of executioners, then a pine coffin carried by four men. Last came the prisoner himself marched in the midst of four guards. Finally, a number of men, under arrest for various offenses, were brought out in hope that the moral affect of this spectacle would leave a lasting impression.

When the procession reached the open side of the hollow square, the men wheeled to the left and marched all along the inside of the line, from right to left, with the band still playing the dirge. After having solemnly traversed the entire length of the three sides of the hollow square, the procession came to the open side, opposite the point from which they had started. The escort wheeled off. The prisoner was placed before his coffin which was set down in front of his grave. The squad of twelve men who were to shoot the deserter positioned themselves some ten or twelve yards from the grave and faced the prisoner. A chaplain stepped out from the group of division officers nearby and prayed with and for the prisoner. The division bugler then sounded, and an officer in charge of the squad stepped forward. Gus heard the command given as calmly as if on drill:

Ready! Aim!

Then, drowning out the third command, *Fire!*, came a flash of smoke and a loud report. Gus jumped in his skin. The deserter fell backwards, riddled with bloody holes. The surgeons examined the corpse, and the band now struck up a quickstep. The entire division was marched past the corpse. This was to confirm that the fate of all deserters was death.

Company front.

Two sergeants play cards while a youthful drummer looks on.

Chapter Five

During the early months of 1862, General George McClellan devised a daring and bold plan to attack and capture the Confederate Capital of Richmond from the southeast. The Army of the Potomac was to be transported by sea to Fortress Monroe for an advance up the lightly defended Virginia Peninsula.

The 40th New York Infantry (Mozart Regiment) was in the Second Brigade, commanded by General David B. Birney, of General Charles S. Hamilton's Third Division, of General Samuel Heintzelman's Third Army Corps.

On February 4, 1862, Gus observed his thirteenth birthday and after morning roll-call the members of the drum corps celebrated the event by giving him a blanket toss.

Gus's comrades slowly surrounded him and before he could remonstrate he was seized bodily and thrown headlong upon a big blanket, held by several stout men. The blanket hung slack in the middle.

—One! Two! Three! Hip!

The men pulled the blanket taut, and launched Gus ten feet in the air.

—Again!

Twelve feet in the air.

—Again!

Fifteen feet in the air.

—Happy birthday, Gustav! the soldiers all shouted and cheered, and then threw another hapless drummer into the blanket.

Later that afternoon, a large box arrived from home by

express, in which was very neatly packed a woolen shirt, socks, soap, and a towel, along with many delicious surprises: a well-roasted chicken, cheese, pudding, pickles, potatoes, onions, toothsome preserves, dried apples, tea, and a can of condensed milk. Gus was in heaven. He ate his fill and shared the rest with his pards.

On Monday, March 17th, the spring campaign was officially underway. The day of departure was remarkably fair. The skies were bright, and the air was warm and balmy. The Mozart Regiment, along with the other regiments in the brigade, marched to the Alexandria docks where they began boarding vessels for the Virginia Peninsula.

As their steamer drifted down the Potomac River the Mozarters passed Mount Vernon, George Washington's home and final resting place. Gus admired the stately mansion with its row of white pillars, beautifully situated on high ground just a quarter mile back from the riverside. Gus remembered his school days when he was taught about the Father of Our Country. All of the Mozarters held George Washington in great reverence and the soldiers uncovered their heads as they passed Mount Vernon.

Five gunboats followed alongside the steamers as an escort which periodically fired into the woods to dislodge any hidden Rebel artillery that might have been positioned there. That night, the men slept in bunks while they serenely continued down to the Chesapeake Bay.

It was raining hard when the 40th New York disembarked at Fortress Monroe. The men marched to their assigned camp and put up their tents with difficulty, since everything was soaking wet. Each Mozarter carried a six-by-four-foot piece of canvas called a "shelter-half." Gus and Tommy Connolly buttoned their shelter-halves together to make a tent. This tent was then thrown over a pole held up by two crotched sticks about three feet in height, which were stuck in the ground six feet apart. The tent was then staked down to the ground on each side. The two boys fit comfortably inside. They closed the ends with their rubber blankets and put some boards down on the wet ground to keep themselves out of the mud. They then put one woolen blanket down to cover the boards, and the other was used to cover themselves. Their knapsacks served as pillows. Despite the rain, they were very comfortable.

—Oh, I tell you Gus, said Tommy, but isn't this solid comfort? There's many a poor fellow in the world who hasn't such a nice, comfortable bed as this, eh?

—This may look like a rat hole, replied Gus, but I feel like a king in a palace.

When morning came it was still raining and everyone did their best to dry themselves in front of huge campfires fueled by burning fence rails. The foragers had gone out early and had returned with an abundance of rabbits and wild hogs. After a few days the weather turned warm and dry, and they were soon on the march again.

The Third Corps was ordered to march to Yorktown, about thirty miles away, where the Confederate army was entrenched. The 40th New York arrived at the outskirts of Yorktown on Saturday, March 29th, with the enemy in sight. The Mozarters were tired and hungry. Their ration wagons were ten miles to the rear and stuck in the mud. Some of the men were allowed to hunt for wild hogs, and in a short time they all had something to eat.

The siege of Yorktown had begun and the following four weeks were spent in the trenches, digging and building forts, under the constant fire of Rebel artillery and sharpshooters. Sometime during the siege, a member of Company I sent the following poem to the *New York Sunday Mercury*:

TO THE MOZART (FORTIETH REGIMENT N.Y.S.V.)

The night is dark and dismal,
And black clouds seem to frown
On the lonely Mozart picket
Near the forts of old Yorktown.

Cheer up, brave boys, 'twill soon depart,
The cloud that there doth frown
Is vapor from a rebel's heart
That slumbers near Yorktown.

Keep close watch on that dark wood there,
And stand behind this tree—
Boom, boom, it burst up in the air—
That shell was meant for me.

They feed again the cannon's mouth,
Quick, boys, aim and fire—
Bang, bravo! bravo! Mozart pickets,
You've rolled them in the mire.

Watch ye well their rebel sports
Until that sun looks down.
Whose rays shall glisten on our flag
In the heart of old Yorktown.

Brave Mozarts, fight ye till the last,
Quick leap their breastworks o'er.
When speaks the signal-trumpet's blast
We'll leave them in their gore.

Thou shalt return to the loved ones
With victory's waving plume,
Or sleep like your brave fathers
In a soldier's glorious tomb.

On Tuesday, April 29th, the drum corps had just finished sounding dinner-call when a Rebel artillery shell exploded close by. Drummer Billy Hayes of Company C was struck a glancing blow on the side of his face by a fragment of the shell and was badly cut. Gus and Tommy slowly lifted Billy to his feet and gave him a drink of water. Colonel Riley, who was nearby, helped the boy to the surgeon's tent where they bandaged his head. Billy's shoulder was also bruised, but he declined to go to the hospital and instead remained on duty, proud that he was the first man of the regiment to be wounded by Rebel shot. He had become a hero, and several of the boys even became envious of Billy and his wound.

On the first day of May, the men heard vague rumors that their division commander, General Hamilton, had in some manner displeased General McClellan and was being removed. This was proven true by the issuing of the following order:

HEADQUARTERS, THIRD DIVISION, THIRD CORPS,
GENERAL ORDERS No. 1   YORKTOWN, May 3, 1862.

Pursuant to instructions from Headquarters of the Army and of the Corps Commander, I hearby assume command of the Division, composed of Generals Birney's, Jameson's and Berry's brigades, and of Thompson's, Reams' and Randolph's batteries.
Philip Kearny, Brigadier General, Commanding.

Many of the men had heard of Philip Kearny's gallantry in the Mexican War and his loss of an arm in battle. Amongst the men, the prevailing sentiment was that it was preferable to be commanded by an experienced soldier than by one who had never seen any fighting. With great anticipation the men awaited the arrival of their new general, and when Phil Kearny appeared he proved to be all that they had heard about him--and a great deal more.

The Mozarters' first meeting with the general wasn't entirely enjoyable. The men and officers of the regiment were out on picket duty, but the major, the adjutant, the regimental drum corps, and those who were on the sick list remained in camp. General Kearny had ordered that no campfire should be lit while the enemy was at such close range, lest the light reveal their position. Some of the boys in the drum corps defied the order and began cooking over a blazing fire which could be seen from General Kearny's headquarters. As Gus watched with baited breath, an aide was dispatched to have the fire put out and the wrongdoers brought to punishment. But the drum corps boys, who started the blaze, hooted the aide and went on with their cooking. Kearny then came riding furiously into the camp. Every man, sick or well, turned out in alarm. The drum corps boys scattered in every direction, but the general rode them down and put them to work extinguishing the blaze. He then directed the major and the adjutant to put out the fire, saying that their commissions would not be worth salt if this disobedience of orders ever occurred again.

No more fires were kindled in camp and the boys, thereafter, were models of good behavior when within the possible reach of General Kearny.

The following day the Confederates evacuated Yorktown. The Mozarters were ordered to cautiously advance toward the Rebel lines; but, some of the Mozarters were overeager to be the first to enter the enemy's works and commenced a footrace to the Rebel fort. This upset Colonel Riley, who shouted at the soldiers to get back into ranks, but it was of no use.

As soon as the regiment entered the Rebel fort, they fell into line and the command was given: *Order arms!* Suddenly, a terrific explosion occurred followed by screams and curses. Private George McFarrar's rifle had struck the percussion cap of a twelve-inch bomb buried by the Rebels just beneath the surface of the ground. McFarrar and Private Michael McDermott were killed instantly and three others were severely wounded. Gus saw one man who had his leg completely blown off, and another who had his arm hanging limp and bloody. Other hidden explosives were sought and many were discovered. Later, Confederate prisoners were brought in and were forced to remove the buried explosives.

That evening, while preparing supper, the men swore to avenge the deaths of their comrades in the upcoming fight. Their battle-cry would be: "Death to the Rebels!"

Because the regiment planned to march before daylight in pursuit of the retreating Confederate army, no one pitched their shelter tents. That night it rained. Gus awakened with the rain falling on his face. He pulled his india-rubber blanket over his head, and in his drowsiness began to think of home and his mother and father. Soon he fell into a deep sleep and began to dream of home. It was suppertime. His mother was preparing a delicious, sweet-smelling meal: freshly baked bread, butter, ham, cheese, cakes, and milk. She smiled and petted his forehead and asked God to protect her boy; then she began to weep. Frederick looked deathly ill. He was sitting in his chair; his face was pale and drawn. Mother's weeping was becoming mournful and the sweet dream was twisting into a nightmare. Papa was dying before his eyes. Gus looked into his father's hollow eye sockets and remembered his words: Do your whole duty, my son. Then Gus felt a light tap on his shoulder, and was awakened from his dream.

The adjutant was tapping Gus with his sword.

—Wake up, soldier. The colonel has ordered reveille.

The morning was cold, wet, and very disagreeable. Gus rubbed his eyes and reached for his bugle in the darkness. He could not locate it. It was gone! In a panic, he felt wildly around through his blankets and knapsack until he remembered that he had stuffed the bugle inside his haversack to keep it dry. A few seconds later, the bugle's waking echoes quickly brought the men to their feet, and they hurriedly began to gather their equipment. Gustav slung the bugle cord over his shoulder and vowed never to be separated from the instrument again.

Breakfast consisted of only a few hardtack crackers. As they finished their meal, Gus could hear the thunder of distant artillery. The Confederates were making a stand near Williamsburg and the battle that the Mozarters had wished for so fervently had begun.

—*Fall in, Company I!* yelled Sergeant Brady. Pack up immediately! We have orders to move!

—Where are we going? asked a dozen voices.

—We go where they tell us to go, and in light marching order! No knapsacks; only a gum blanket and three days' rations in your haversacks; and be lively now! shouted the sergeant.

It was not long before they were ready with thirty pieces of hardtack, a piece of pork; a little coffee and sugar in their haversacks; gum blankets rolled and slung over their shoulders. All the drummers belonging to the regiment gathered and began tightening their drums and tuning them with a tap-tap-tap of the drumstick. They took position and, at the adjutant's signal, beat the assembly. At the first sound of the long roll, the whole regiment formed a line of two ranks, then turned into a column of fours. A cheer went up, for the monotony of siege life was plainly at an end, and the Mozarters were finally going into their first battle. All the while, the rain continued to fall.

Because the rain saturated the drumheads and rendered them useless, the boys slung them over their shoulders as the order was given: *Forward--route-step--march!*

The soldiers always welcomed the order "route-step," a step in which each man picks his own stride, carrying or shifting his arms at will. Even then the march was not easy; especially in the rain with the course being through deep, sticky, Virginia clay mud. When Gus set one foot down, he could scarcely pull the other one out.

—There goes one of my shoes, cried Tommy Connolly, as his shoe was sucked from his foot.

—Talk about mud in New York! said Corporal Brown. Pshaw! You never saw any mud in New York in comparison with this!

The Mozart Regiment marched toward the sound of the guns thundering at Williamsburg. Kearny's division had been ordered to the front to assist General Joe Hooker's division, which had been fighting the enemy since early morning. The Mozarters passed thousands of soldiers who were halted in the fields by the roadside. Corporal Brown called to some and asked if they had been in the fight. They all responded, "No."

The Mozarters began to wonder aloud why these thousands of men were idly lying along the roadside and not going into the battle.

—This is OUR fight boys, announced Corporal Brown. Remember McFarrar and McDermott!

During this march, Gus saw entire batteries of artillery become mired in the mud. He observed one cannon stuck in a deep mud hole and twenty men trying to pull it out. Farther along the road, a merchant wagon, belonging to a regimental sutler, blocked their path. With a bellowing voice, General Kearny threatened to put it to the torch if the merchant did not get out of the way. Needless to say, the driver hauled it off to the roadside as quickly as possible. The men in the ranks cheered Kearny for cursing the sutler and added a few choice words of their own.

As the Mozarters drew closer to the battlefield, they could plainly see an open field outstretched before them, and farther away a barricade of felled timber behind which some Rebels had taken cover. In the distance stood the Rebel fort.

General Heintzelman met them near the edge of the battlefield and shouted: "No more Bull Runs, men! No more Bull Runs!" He then ordered the drum corps to play music. "Play! Play! It's all you're good for," he yelled. "Play 'Yankee Doodle,' or any doodle you can think of, only play something!" Despite the wet drumheads, Gus and the drum corps selected a tune and began to play with all their energy. They knew that they needed to inspire the tired infantry as they prepared to advance into battle.

Colonel Riley turned to face the regiment and then shouted: *Load!*

The soldiers quickly handled their paper cartridges, tore them open with their teeth and poured the charge into their muskets. After ramming the ball home, the piece was primed with a percussion cap.

Fix-Bayonets! shouted the colonel.

The rattle and clink of eight hundred bayonets could clearly be heard over notes of *Yankee Doodle.*

Moments later, General Kearny furiously rode up, his horse sending a shower of mud in all directions. Heintzelman suggested that perhaps Kearny better let General Hooker assist, as Kearny was new to his command.

Kearny stared at Heintzelman indignantly for a moment and then grinned.

"General, I can make men follow me to hell."

Kearny turned to Colonel Riley and ordered him to divide the regiment, the colonel commanding five companies in reserve, while Kearny led the rest of the regiment in a charge up the road. The general's order was punctuated by an exploding shell overhead. Some men flinched, but the majority stood firm. Gus was thrilled, yet frightened. His courage would now be tested in battle! Would he be killed? Worse, would he turn tail and run away? What would his comrades do? What would his father say? His young mind raced with questions.

Do your whole duty, he thought to himself as he braced for battle.

From his vantage point, Gus watched General Kearny ride all along the firing line. He could not take his eyes off the conspicuous general as Kearny was constantly directing his troops in person and placing himself in peril. Tommy said that he believed the general led a charmed life as he braved the fusillade of shot and shell without incident.

Kearny spurred his horse into a little clearing and, looking about like an eagle in search of prey, shouted to his men to show themselves and drive the Confederates out of their cover. Responding to his appeal, a few Union skirmishers rose on their side of the felled timber. They had scarcely made their appearance when a whole line of Rebel marksmen jumped to their feet from their lairs, took deliberate aim, and fired simultaneously at General Kearny. They all missed. Kearny laughed and shook his stump of an arm at them. He then galloped away unscathed.

It was a hard fight, but by the end of the day the Confederates retreated and left their dead and wounded behind. Casualties from North and South lay side by side on the bloody battlefield. To Gus, there appeared to be as many Rebels killed as Union men. For the next several hours the boys in the drum corps helped bring the wounded to the field hospital. Nearly all the Union wounded were brought in during the night and then the wounded Rebels received attention.

At daybreak the next morning, Gus and some of the other drummer boys walked across the battlefield. The ground was still soaked by the recent rains, and a heavy shroud-like mist hung over the field, causing the dead to appear all the more ghastly. Some of the deceased looked calm as if asleep; some were still grasping their muskets, with high, defiant looks; others had expressions of agony on their faces. Gus noticed that some died clutching small Testaments or photographs of loved ones. His heart began to ache for his mother. He wished that he had her photograph so that he could look upon her dear face to make this terrible scene before him go away.

—Gustav! Come away from this, said Glass-Put-In. I am sickened by this sight! It is too awful to look at any more!

Gus saw that a squad of men with shovels were now hard at work burying the dead. Most of the men in blue were buried already, and now trenches were being dug for the poor fellows in gray.

The Mozarters took a number of prisoners at Williamsburg. The prisoners were put under guard in a fenced area and given the same rations as Union soldiers. It was the first time that Gus had ever seen a live Rebel. One long-haired Alabamian, about twenty years old, looked very different from the Union soldiers, yet had in his eyes the same determination that Gus had seen in so many of his comrades in blue. Gus overheard one wounded prisoner say that his home was in Alexandria and if he ever returned he would never leave there again; he'd had enough of war. Another Confederate from South Carolina wore an elaborate gray uniform with fancy gilt buttons emblazoned with a palmetto tree under which appeared the Latin motto, *Animis opibusque parati*--"Prepared in mind and resources." When Sergeant Brady asked the meaning of the motto, the prisoner retorted, "It means: 'Give the damned Yankees fits.'"

Kearny's division left Williamsburg after a few days' rest. The rest of the army continued its march up the peninsula towards Richmond, passing many farms and plantations along the way. It seemed that at every halt a search would begin for something to eat. Smokehouses, hen roosts...no building was safe from the "Forty Thieves."

One afternoon, while marching past a plantation, the drum corps struck up some lively music. The colonel noticed that Gus was not beating his drum.

—Adjutant, said the displeased colonel, one of the drummers is not beating. Go, and find the reason why.

Riding up to the drum corps, the adjutant, with a frown on his face, shouted:

—You there!

Gus looked up.

—The colonel wants to know why you are not beating your drum.

—Tell the colonel that I can't beat my drum now.

—May I tell him why not? the adjutant demanded, finding no humor in the situation.

—Tell him that I have two live chickens inside my drum and one of them is for the colonel!

The march dragged on for days and, despite the songs and jokes, it became a memorably tedious and unpleasant event. On Saturday, May 10th, the Mozarters marched ten miles, bringing them within forty-five miles of Richmond. By Thursday, May 15th, they reached Cumberland, only twenty-five miles from Richmond. The weather turned hot and the roads dusty. During the long march to White House Landing on the Pamunkey River, all suffered a great deal from thirst. Good, clean water was non-existent. During the frequent rain showers, the soldiers would stop and drink from muddy puddles in the road. At one place where water was particularly scarce, Gus saw some soldiers crowding around a mud puddle drinking heartily, while on the other side of the puddle lay a dead mule.

Upon arriving at their designated camp for the evening, the soldiers made a grand rush for the nearest rail fences and began dismantling them. In no time at all, miles of Virginia rail fence were distributed, and hundreds of campfires blazed throughout the encampment. After building a fire, a soldier's first task was to cook his tin cup of coffee, a beverage considered as indispensable as the very air. A cup of strong, black coffee, ofttimes made of muddy ditch water, did more to recuperate and cheer a cold, wet, tired, and travel-worn soldier than a person could ever imagine.

The Mozart Regiment rested at White House Landing for several days. The area was swampy and very unhealthy. Many became ill with malaria or "swamp fever." When steamers came up the river from Washington with supplies for the army, they also brought sutlers with exorbitantly-priced wares. Gus bought a loaf of white bread and Tommy paid seventy-five cents for some butter, and the two pards enjoyed a feast. Glass-Put-In purchased the latest edition of *Harper's Weekly*, and he read aloud to the boys about the great battle General Ulysses Grant had won at a place in Tennessee called Pittsburg Landing, also known as Shiloh. The news of this victory, along with a prevailing thought that the war could soon be over, uplifted their spirits.

REVEILLE.

Chapter Six

The Army of the Potomac was now only seven miles from the Capital of the Confederacy. Some Federal pickets could even see the church spires of Richmond. The confidence of the Mozarters was unbounded, with many believing that the Federals would capture the city within a week and that the war would be over by the end of June.

During the afternoon of Saturday, May 31st, Gus and his comrades heard the sound of distant musketry increasing steadily, and they anticipated another battle. Soon Gus saw dozens, then hundreds, of retreating Union soldiers dash by--just as before at Bull Run! General Silas Casey's 12,000 men, who had been the lead division, were being driven back and the Third Corps, held in reserve, was ordered up to stop the Rebel advance.

General Birney detached the 40th New York from the brigade and placed the regiment in an open field bordering thick woods near a place called Seven Pines. The woods reverberated with the roar and crash of thousands of muskets and cannon. Colonel Riley, mounted on a spirited charger, formed the regiment in a line of battle. The drum corps was positioned directly behind the colors at the center of the line. While waiting for orders to advance, General Kearny emerged from the woods and rode up in front of their line and called to them:

"Wait, my brave Mozarters, I'll soon have you in it, for there's lots of good fighting all along the line."

The men cheered. They found Kearny inspirational and charismatic, and were prepared to follow him anywhere.

Colonel Riley held his sword aloft, then shouted the command:

"Mozarters! Forward, march!"

The men stepped off as the drums beat the pace, and another cheer rose up from the ranks. Confederate skirmishers opened a brisk fire at the Mozarters and many fell wounded, but the regiment pressed on. After entering the woods, Colonel Riley's horse suddenly became frenzied and uncontrollable. The colonel was thrown violently to the ground and knocked unconscious. The surgeon quickly called for a stretcher. Gus stared solemnly as the litter-bearers lifted the colonel and carried him to the rear. Lieutenant-Colonel Thomas Egan was now in command of the regiment.

The Third Corps checked the Rebel advance that afternoon, and darkness ended the day's battle. Both sides were busy throughout the night strengthening their lines, and as a result no Mozarter was permitted to leave the ranks for any cause. The men had to go without any supper or breakfast.

The fighting was renewed early the next morning. The 40th New York was positioned next to an old log house near the edge of an orchard. At around eight o'clock, a strong Rebel line advanced upon them with their blood-red flags waving. The air then immediately filled with bullets and exploding shells and several soldiers dropped to the ground with ghastly wounds. Colonel Egan ordered the drummers to lay aside their drums and hurry to the ambulances in the rear; stretchers were needed to carry the wounded off the line of battle. Gus was so mesmerized by the advancing Confederates that he did not hear the colonel's command. He silently watched as the gray line continued to advance with perfect precision. It was truly a magnificent sight. At a distance of one hundred yards the Rebels halted and began to fire by files. Gus heard the bullets buzz overhead and thought that they sounded like a swarm of angry bees.

Colonel Egan soon spotted the lone drummer and shouted to him to hurry with the stretchers.

Gus snapped out of his trance and reacted. He unhooked his

drum, dropped his knapsack, and ran towards the ambulances some three hundred yards to the rear. Gus and Tommy picked up a stretcher and headed back to the line of battle. They could see the regimental colors in the distance waving beyond the orchard near the log house.

When they arrived at the orchard, Gus counted four men of Company I lying on the ground wounded. Among them lay a tall, magnificently-built man in a colorful Zouave uniform. To Gus, the man appeared to be sleeping. He looked very calm lying on his back at full length with his musket beside him. Then Gus noticed the fatal bloody mark on the soldier's forehead and the ashen pallor of death on his face. He stared at the dead Zouave for a moment, then turned to watch Private George Miller who was loading and firing his musket as fast as he could, while singing at the top of his voice. All of a sudden, Miller swore with pain. He was hit in the leg with some buckshot and commenced hopping and cursing up a storm. Gus leaned into him and helped Miller to sit down, uncorking his canteen for him.

—Gustav! shouted Tommy, for God's sake, come over here!

Gus left Miller and hurried to the side of his pard who was giving water to a captain whose arm had been taken off near the shoulder. As blood poured from the wound, the two boys lay the officer down on the stretcher and Gus began to apply a tourniquet. He worked quickly to stem the flow of blood and desperately watched as the captain's face grew white.

Two stout privates arrived and lifted the stretcher, as the captain spoke gratefully to Gus and Tommy:

—Thanks, my friends. Thanks to you I shall see my mother again.

Gus looked at his hands; they were covered with the captain's blood. He took out a dirty handkerchief and gingerly wiped his bloody fingers. As the battle continued to rage on, Tommy realized that there was not going to be enough stretchers for all of the wounded men. Gus suggested that since the rear of the log house offered some protection from musketry, they should assist the wounded to the shelter of the building. After helping some of the injured to safety, Gus began hearing a long high-pitched yell coming from the Rebel lines. The howling grew in intensity and began to panic some of the wounded men. Curiously creeping around the corner of the house, Gus saw long lines of gray advancing towards them, all howling the terrifying yell.

 —Here they come, boys! someone shouted. We'll have to go at them on a charge!

 Colonel Egan then placed a cautious hand on Gus's shoulder.

 —Keep back, my boy; no use exposing yourself in that way.

A bayonet charge was ordered and as the men fixed bayonets, Gus and the other drummers ran to retrieve their drums a few yards away. Suddenly, a shell shrieked by and plunged into the ground near Gus smashing his drum to tatters and plowing up a great furrow under Tommy who had been standing nearby. The two shaken boys stood and stared at the torn earth and shattered remains of the drum. Tommy turned to face Gus and winked.

 —Well, pard, that was certainly a close shave, wasn't it?

 —Yes it was, indeed.

 —At least you still have your bugle.

The Rebels increased their fire at the Mozarters and the noise became deafening. Colonel Egan grabbed Gus by the collar and positioned him behind the regimental colors. He ordered him to keep his bugle at the ready, and to wait for the command to signal the charge. Gus unslung his bugle and wrapped the cord several times around his forearm. The colonel then pressed through the color guard and took position at the head of the regiment. Sword held high, he shouted above the din:

 "Mozarters! Charge bayonets! Charge!"

Gus brought the bugle to his lips and sounded the advance. The regiment hurrahed and started at the double-quick. Gus sprinted along with the flag-bearers as fast as his short legs could go. He followed Color Sergeant Joseph Conroy with the national banner waving high overhead. Then Gus saw Conroy fall. A bullet had pierced Conroy's brain, killing him instantly. Corporal Charles Boyle then grabbed the colors, and seconds later he too was fatally shot. As Boyle fell, Corporal Tommy Breslin seized the flag before it touched the ground and in a few moments he too lay bleeding and disabled by a vicious leg wound.

The flag was down. Gus reached for the flagstaff, but in an instant he felt himself lifted from his feet, spun around, and thrown heavily to the ground.

—Oh, God! he gasped. Have I been shot?

The dazed boy sat up, caught his breath, and felt for the dreaded wound. Strangely enough, there was no pain. Looking at his legs and arms, and feeling them, Gus wondered aloud:

—No blood? No wound? Thank God!

Bewildered, Gus slowly rose to his feet and peered through the smoke for his regiment. The charge had pressed on without him.

The Rebels, not relishing the idea of cold steel, had turned and fled. The Mozarters charged the enemy to the edge of a wooded area where they were met by a heavy fire from the front and left. They could advance no further. It was here that the storyteller, Gilbert Abrams, was shot through the body.

—I am a dead man, boys! he exclaimed, but it's for the Union! Go in and give the damn Rebels fits!

Abrams died a few moments later.

The Mozarters slowly fell back to their original position and the wounded were carried off. Gus rejoined the regiment as it was reforming. Glass-Put-In thought Gus had been killed in the charge and expressed wonder, then joy, at seeing him alive.

—Gustav! My God! I thought you were dead for sure! exclaimed Glass-Put-In.

—No, not so bad as that, said Gus.

—What in blazes happened to you? asked Tommy.

—I'm not quite sure. I was on my feet one moment and then flat on my back the next. It was the most peculiar feeling...like someone had grabbed me by the arm and threw me to the ground.

Scattered about were groups of men discussing the battle and relating exciting incidents and adventures of the fray. One fellow pointed proudly to the bullet holes in his cap and coat. Another showed that his cartridge box had been pierced by a bullet. Yet another fellow laughed as he held up his punctured canteen calling it a "trophy of war."

All of these observations were unsettling for Gus, who was amazed that men could still laugh and joke with this macabre sense of humor.

—Gustav, what happened to your drum? asked Corporal Brown knowingly.

—Smashed to bits, came the reply.

—Better the drum than you, laughed the corporal. What happened to your bugle?

Gus pulled the cord from his shoulder and began turning the bugle around in his hands. He at once saw that the mouthpiece had been completely shot away. A Rebel bullet had cut it cleanly off and the force of the shot had thrown Gus to the ground.

—So that's what made me fall!

—Well pard, there's another close shave for you, grinned Tommy. Now you have a trophy of war to send your father.

The Battle of Seven Pines ended at dusk on June 1st, and was considered a tactical draw. More than 11,000 men were killed, wounded or missing. Gus had often seen pictures of battlefields and had read about them, and he had even witnessed the field after the battle at Williamsburg. But the most terrible scenes of carnage his boyish imagination had ever conjured up fell far short of the dreadful reality that he beheld after the Battle of Seven Pines. Dead men were everywhere, and hundreds of dead horses created a sickening stench. Dismounted gun carriages, shattered caissons, knapsacks, haversacks, muskets, bayonets, accoutrements were all scattered over the field in the wildest confusion. That night, details were busily engaged in burying the dead in long trenches.

Early the next morning, General McClellan visited General Heintzelman's Third Corps headquarters. Gus watched McClellan ride up to a soldier, whose arm was in a sling, and asked if he was seriously hurt. McClellan then dismounted and shook hands with the leading generals who had been in the fight: Heintzelman, Kearny, Hooker, Sedgwick; all had pleasant smiles on their faces. Heintzelman knelt down on one knee and marked out on the ground his role in the battle. The others stood around him in a circle. When he told of some important movement, he looked up at McClellan who nodded his head and smiled. It was an impressive sight to Gus, seeing so many distinguished generals together at the same time.

Gus and his comrades remained on the edge of the battlefield on the following day, Tuesday, June 3rd. The doctors in the army hospital sent word that Colonel Riley had suffered a severe head injury from his fall and was being sent home to recover. It was certainly a sad fate for the commander to be separated from the men he had faithfully and patiently transformed into proficient soldiers. Gus considered this a personal loss, for it was Colonel Riley who had given him the chance to be a soldier.

All was quiet again. The Mozarters resumed picket duty and kept a watchful eye on the Confederate lines. A captured Rebel picket confirmed the rumors about the wounding of the Confederate Army's commander, General Joseph Johnston, at Seven Pines, and the prisoner said that another general now had command. His name was General Robert E. Lee.

Colonel Thomas Egan of the 40th New York.

Chapter Seven

After the Battle of Seven Pines, inaction prevailed between the two armies for several weeks until Wednesday, June 25th. General McClellan ordered the Third Corps to advance their pickets closer towards Richmond, and the enemy stubbornly resisted the attempt. The brief engagement, called the Battle of Oak Grove, lasted only about two hours. The Confederate Army of Northern Virginia, under General Robert E. Lee, then launched a counterstroke which resulted in a week-long struggle, called the Seven Days' Battles, June 25 to July 1, 1862.

Being a musician without any instruments, Gus volunteered for duty assisting the surgeons in their bloody work at the field hospital after the Battle of Oak Grove. The temporary hospital was actually located in an old dilapidated barn. The doctors were kept busy throughout the night, as there were about 500 casualties from Hooker's and Kearny's divisions.

The scene inside the barn reminded Gus of a slaughter house he had once seen in New York. He watched in horror as dozens of wounded soldiers had limbs sawed off, many with only the benefit of whiskey after the supply of chloroform was depleted. Gus was astounded that the surgeons appeared to be so unaffected by the patients' wailing, moaning, and screaming. This field hospital seemed far different from the hospital in Georgetown where he had visited his father.

The surgeons operated with their shirt sleeves rolled up, and their aprons were red with blood, as if they were butchers.

Upon a board laid across two barrels, a young soldier was outstretched. A surgeon was about to amputate the shattered mass of flesh that was once a leg. The doctor impatiently called for assistance from the orderlies as he was very fatigued from working long hours with no rest. An assistant held a candle aloft providing barely adequate light for the doctor to perform the operation. The sight and sound of the leg bone being sawed mixed with the screams of the patient almost caused Gus to retch as he stood there with an armful of bandages. His head was spinning. The surgeon hurriedly bound up the leg in a routine-like fashion, and then he ordered Gus to take a bucket and fetch some more water from the well.

Running from the barn into the pitch-black darkness, Gus stumbled and landed into a heap. Grasping about in order to steady himself, he caught hold of something wet and slimy. He had fallen into a large pile of human legs and arms that had just been amputated. As he frantically scrambled to climb out of the slippery, bloody, hideous mass of cold flesh, a dozen hands seemed to grasp at him.

Gus quickly rolled out of the bloody muck and rose to his feet. He was badly shaken. Picking up the bucket, he continued to the well and splashed his face with water several times.

A wild shriek then emanated from one of the operating tables inside the barn.

—Oh, doctor! Kill me and be done with it! Kill me, and put me out of my misery!

The shrieking made Gus shudder. He took a deep breath, wiped his brow and went back to work. He pitied the men brought here, as there was little anyone could do to alleviate their pain and suffering.

On Thursday, June 26th, Robert E. Lee took the offensive and launched a maneuver to destroy the Army of the Potomac. Lee ordered an attack upon the Union Fifth Corps near the village of Mechanicsville, and again the following day at Gaines's Mill.

For the next four days the two armies fought constantly; the Confederates attacking during the day, and the Federals retreating during the night.

Gus and the soldiers in the Third Corps field hospital heard distant firing to their right and rear. They believed the Rebels were trying to turn the Union flank and drive them away from the front of Richmond.

General McClellan's nerve failed. He was under the impression that his army was heavily outnumbered, and he ordered a hasty retreat south to Harrison's Landing on the James River. While McClellan referred to this order as a "change of base," the men in the ranks dubbed it the "Great Skedaddle." General Kearny and his soldiers were displeased by this order, seeing it as a retreat in the face of the enemy, but they were still determined to fight and whip the Rebels. During the retreat, Kearny's division was assigned the post of danger and responsibility as the rear guard of the entire Army of the Potomac.

All of the wounded in the field hospital who could not walk had to be left behind. Gus thought it awful the way the poor fellows begged to be taken along. It just could not be done. He knew that most of them would die, for the Rebels could not even take care of their own wounded.

On June 29th, Gus rejoined the Mozarters as they prepared to retreat south to the James River. The Federals evacuated Savage's Station, leaving 2,500 wounded behind. At the station, Gus watched in fascination as carloads of ammunition were blown up to prevent it from falling into the hands of the enemy. As they continued the retreat, many of the soldiers collapsed from exhaustion after days of fighting and marching without rest. When they halted, even for a moment, the soldiers dropped in the road and fell so soundly asleep that it was difficult to rouse them.

On the morning of June 30th, the Mozart Regiment ate their breakfast of hardtack and coffee, and had everything ready for their march before daylight.

The Mozarters marched a short distance and formed in a line of battle on the edge of an open field, awaiting the enemy. There were plenty of blackberry bushes nearby, and some of the men asked for permission to gather berries. The officers told them they must not go far, and to return the instant they heard the drums. Gus went along and picked a quantity of berries, which tasted sweet and delicious. It was a welcome treat as he had eaten nothing but hardtack for days. Just as he was starting to have his fill, the drums beat and all ran back to their places.

The Confederate assault began at four o'clock in the afternoon against Kearny's division along the Charles City Crossroad. The ferocious attacks were repulsed by effective infantry and artillery fire. The Confederates were literally being cut down by the hundreds, but the strategic importance of capturing this crossroad caused them to increase their efforts. Artillery shells were flying about in a lively fashion, and one shell exploded near General Kearny's horse. Some of the Mozarters dodged behind trees to avoid being in the path of danger. General Kearny rebuked them:

"Get back in line! Those shells don't hurt me, and they won't hurt you."

Then, another shell exploded directly above and a small fragment hit General Kearny in the breast without causing him any injury. He coolly remarked:

"It is evident that the enemy would as soon hit a fellow, as not."

The Confederates charged again, right into the muzzles of Federal cannons, and the iron canister balls cut great swaths through their lines. Gus had never seen such bloody slaughter; it was even worse than the carnage at Williamsburg or Seven Pines.

Kearny's division held firm. The firing ceased as darkness fell, but there was no time to rest or sleep. At midnight, the exhausted Federals continued their retreat to Harrison's Landing. They marched until daylight when they arrived at Malvern Hill--a place well adapted for defense.

On the seventh and final day of the battles, the Mozart Regiment was detailed to support an artillery battery near the foot of the slope of Malvern Hill. For Gus and the rest of the infantry it was a grand sight to see these artillerymen in action, steady and regular as the stroke of machinery. How skillfully one man handled the sponge-staff, while runners brought up the little red bag of powder and the long, conical shell from the caisson in the rear. How swiftly they rammed them home! The lieutenant sighted his piece, then the man with the lanyard--with a sudden jerk--fired the primer, and the gun leapt five feet to the rear. Out of the cannon's throat in a cloud of smoke rushed the shell, shrieking its message of death into the enemy lines a mile-and-a-half away. The Mozarters rendered the air with hurrahs, for the Rebel's fire had been answered.

An artillery duel ensued that kept the air quivering and quaking for an hour-and-a-half. To Gus, the battle was more exciting because he could see the rhythmic drill of the batteries, with that steady swabbing and ramming, running and sighting, and BANG! BANG! BANG!

It was expected that the Confederates would attack the Mozarters' portion of the line during the afternoon. At one time, General Kearny told Colonel Egan that the Rebels would pay them a visit in about five minutes. The soldiers stayed on edge with the anticipation of an imminent fight. However, the Rebels did not comply, as the attack was executed far to the left of the Mozart Regiment. The Confederate attack failed and the Battle of Malvern Hill was a Federal victory.

Though the Army of the Potomac had been saved from annihilation, the hope of capturing Richmond and ending the war that summer was now forgotten.

General Phil Kearny.

Chapter Eight

In the early hours of July 2nd, the Army of the Potomac continued its retreat to Harrison's Landing, where they were under the protection of Federal gunboats. The soldiers hurriedly built earthworks and remained alert all night expecting another Rebel attack, but it did not come. The exhausted men soon settled down and resumed camp life. It was not long before order and routine were restored with activities such as boiling coffee, washing clothes, reading books and newspapers, and writing letters.

On the Fourth of July, 1862, it had been exactly one year since Gus had last seen his mother and sisters. He borrowed a pen, some ink, and a piece of stationery and wrote a letter home to inform his family that he was safe and well after the previous battles.

On Monday, July 7th, it was announced at morning formation that President Lincoln would be coming from Washington to review the army. Later that afternoon, Corporal Brown, who was now serving as a clerk in General Kearny's headquarters, approached Gus.

—The general has ordered me to get a drummer from our regiment to serve as his orderly for the review tomorrow. Report yourself to division headquarters after roll-call.

—Me? You're joking! Why me?

—Why not you? replied Corporal Brown. The general wants a drummer and you're the best drummer I know.

Gus was thrilled and a little nervous. He spent the rest of the day cleaning and repairing his uniform, which had become dirty and torn in the recent battles. Borrowing a needle and thread from his pard, he sewed the seat of his trousers, then replaced a missing button on his coat. Using some ash from the campfire, Gus did his best to polish his brass buckle and buttons.

Gus reported early the next morning to General Kearny's headquarters. He walked up to the canvas headquarters tent and saluted a captain of Kearny's staff standing outside.

—To which regiment do you belong? asked the captain, returning the salute.

—Fortieth New York, sir, replied Gus.

—A Mozarter! The General will be pleased, said the captain.

At that moment, General Philip Kearny walked out of his tent, elegantly dressed in full uniform, holding his sword and belt. Gus was dazzled by the shiny gold buttons that gleamed in the morning sunlight. Kearny was of medium height, in his mid-forties, and resembled a knight from days of yore. He wore his French-styled kepi tilted jauntily on one side of his head. His fancy cape was thrown over one shoulder, a bright golden-yellow sash tied about his waist, and the empty left sleeve pinned to his breast. Everything about him reflected a leader that men would willingly follow.

—Good morning, sir, Gus saluted.

—Good morning, my lad, replied the general. What is your name?

—Gustav Schurmann, Company I, Fortieth New York Infantry, reporting for duty as orderly for the review, sir.

Kearny then handed Gus his sword and belt and a glove, saying:

—Please help me with this. I hope that you may never lose an arm, for it is impossible to put on a glove without assistance. Can you ride?

—Yes, sir! Gus replied, knowing very well that his only

horseback riding experience was limited to taking the colonel's horse to water.

—Come with me, then, said the general.

The general and Gus walked to the rear of the headquarters tent where three or four horses had been tied to a hitching post. A groomsman was currying a beautiful white mare.

—James! called General Kearny. My orderly here will ride *Baby* today, and I will be riding *Bayard*.

—Yes, sir, General, replied James.

—Baby was brought home from the Mexican War, Kearny said as he patted the mare. She is spirited, so be sure to stay with her.

Several staff officers rode up and informed the general that it was time to proceed to the reviewing field which was a few miles away.

—Gentlemen, prepare to ride like the devil, announced Kearny with glee.

Gus needed help climbing into the saddle. He could scarcely stretch his short legs over Baby's back. But Gus was not alone in his difficulties, for General Kearny, being one-armed, also needed assistance in mounting his horse. Once in the saddle, however, Kearny was the best rider Gus had ever seen.

The general, with his staff and orderly trailing behind, galloped swiftly over rough fields until he came upon a very large ditch. Without hesitation, Kearny spurred his steed to hurdle this formidable obstacle, then glanced over his shoulder to see if any of his aides would dare follow. Dismayed by the jump that the general had just made, the members of his staff changed direction and hunted for an easier and safer crossing.

Only one of the group followed the general's daring feat. Baby was a stablemate of Kearny's horse, and when the general galloped his mount towards the yawning precipice, Baby followed. Gus thought he might as well have tried to stop a railroad train than to check the headlong course of the excited animal. On and on thundered the white charger--ears back, nostrils wide, and eyes ablaze, to the edge of the ravine. Then, rising on her powerful haunches, as if shot from a cannon, she leaped high into the air and safely landed on the other side of the ditch. The daring feat rendered Gus pale and almost breathless.

"Well done! Well done! Good jump!" the general exclaimed proudly.

Later, after the review, when Gus requested permission to return to his regiment, Kearny said, "No, but go and bring your baggage over to headquarters, and consider yourself my orderly in the future."

Gus was stunned. The general said this in such a matter-of-fact manner that Gus was caught off guard. He stood dumbfounded, then beamed with pride. Never did he imagine that General Phil Kearny would ever select him for this important post.

Gus returned to the Mozart camp and secured his knapsack, and all his comrades in the drum corps came to wish him well in his new assignment.

—Lucky fellow! said Glass-Put-In with envy. Orderly to General Kearny! He is the idol of the army.

—Pard, said Tommy, let me give you some free advice: You better keep on your toes day and night for there is no peace for the laggard under Kearny. The cry--*Kearny is coming*--wakes up the men and officers quicker than if it were the enemy.

—Imagine, our little bugler a member of General Kearny's headquarters staff! spoke Sergeant Brady. Kearny is the bravest amongst the brave. He is the best general in the army! Once during the change of base, he was surrounded by a half dozen Rebel skirmishers who leveled their pieces at him and cried out, "Surrender! Surrender!" Kearny looked at them a moment and then said with the utmost contempt, "*You* take *me* prisoner? Back to your regiment, you damned hounds!" And to the great surprise of the Rebels, Kearny put spurs to his horse and rode off at full gallop without paying any further attention to them or the bullets they sent after him.

Sergeant Brady turned to shake Gus's hand.

—Your father will be very proud to hear of your new duty.

—Yes, I must write to him as soon as I can.

Though excited about his new duty with the general, Gus felt sad about parting from his comrades in the Mozart Regiment. So much had happened in the past year since his enlistment in Yonkers. They had shared perils and joys alike. He considered them his second family, after all. Gus became overcome with emotion.

—Comrades, thanks for your well-wishes....I...I will never forget the acts of kindness you have shown me....

Gus could no longer make the words come out.

The boys all crowded around him, laughing and hooting. They then slapped Gus on the back, saying:

—Aw! Don't put on any airs, Gustav! Three cheers for the general's new puppy!

The next morning at headquarters, Corporal Brown handed Gus a two-inch square piece of red flannel.

—Sew this red patch on your cap. Kearny has ordered all of us to wear a red badge so that we can be easily recognized as members of his division.

—When did this come about? asked Gus.

—During the Battle of Seven Pines, Kearny encountered some men he assumed were cowardly shirkers going to the rear and cursed them roundly, ordering them to return to their commands. The soldiers informed the general that he was mistaken--they did not belong to his command. Kearny apologized, and then decided to create the necessary means to identify his men in the future; thus the red diamond-shaped patch. And let me tell you something else. Do you know that Kearny is the only general in history to request his men not to cheer him?

 —That's hard to believe, replied Gus.

 —Yes, it's true. He can't ride through camp anymore without being mobbed by his own troops. He issued this order yesterday which says, "the general takes great pleasure in the kind receptions given him whenever he presents himself among the men, but prefers to be allowed to pass quietly and unobserved. Immediately after a battle, he has no objection to a few hearty cheers." How many generals have had to request their men *not* to cheer them?

 —*Orderly! Where the devil are you?* shouted the general from outside, and Gus was up and running.

Gus understood perfectly why Kearny was so idolized by his troops. Kearny was a *follow me* and not a *go ahead boys* type of a general. He led his troops into battle in person, sharing the dangers and perils alongside the private soldier, and his men almost worshiped him for it. Gus never met anyone more militarily knowledgeable or socially cultured than Phil Kearny. The general had lived for many years in Paris and had campaigned with the French army in Africa and Italy, where he was awarded the Legion d' honour by Emperor Napoleon III.

Being wealthy and accustomed to great luxury, the general lived comfortably on campaign. He maintained an extravagant wagon that housed an elaborate field kitchen supervised by a Parisian chef. Kearny spared no expense and always had the finest uniforms, horses, and camp equipment. Gus enjoyed his new surroundings very much, and the better fare especially. His new tentmates welcomed him kindly, but warned him to keep on his toes in front of the general.

One day, General Kearny presented Gus with a beautiful new bugle to replace his old battle-scarred relic. The general faced the bugler and said:

 —Corporal Brown has told me of your musical ability, and also that you were in the forefront of the charge at Seven Pines.

I want such brave soldiers on my staff. Along with your duties as orderly, you are now also chief bugler of this division.

—Thank you, sir! was all Gus could manage to say, marveling at the shiny new instrument.

Later that evening after Tattoo, Gus played Taps; a new call that had just been composed at Harrison's Landing. Gus thought it was hauntingly beautiful. Some of the men called it the "Soldiers' Lullaby," and softly sang along: "Go to sleep, go to sleep..." Before long, Taps was also being played over the graves of the dead to solemnize their final resting place.

Gus stayed awake until late that night writing a long letter to his father and mother, informing them about his new position. Orderly to a major-general! Division bugler! It seemed to him a tremendous responsibility for a thirteen-year-old boy. It was now his duty to stay beside the general at all times and relay his verbal commands to the entire division by bugle call.

Each morning while in camp at Harrison's Landing, it was General Kearny's custom to ride through the woods outside the picket guards' position, as he was always anxious to know the enemy's whereabouts. Gus always had a difficult time keeping up with the general's rapid pace. Many times Gus would ride lying on top of the horse, lengthwise, so as not to knock his legs against the trees. During one particular ride, Gus had his hat knocked off by a low branch and by the time he retrieved his hat and was in the saddle again, there was no general to be seen. Gus was not sure what to do. If he called out for the general, the Rebels might hear.

—Let's go, Baby. Take me to the general.

Gus gave Baby her own way, and in less than five minutes she brought him to Kearny.

—Damn it, boy, you must keep up, said General Kearny in a low tone. There are Rebels in these woods and they will gobble you up if you are not careful!

Gus did not mind the stern lecture from the irritated general.

Nor did he mind other instances in which Kearny chastised him. Occasionally, when Baby would try to kick at the general, Kearny would "damn" Gus for not keeping the horse under control. But aside from that, the general treated his bugler with soldierly respect.

On one particularly long July day, the temperature on the peninsula was soaring. Kearny and his little bugler, looking very much like a knight and his page, were riding down a dusty road returning from their daily reconnaissance when they encountered Generals Heintzelman and Hooker, who informed them that they were on their way to an "elegant hardtack supper" at the headquarters of Brigadier-General Daniel Sickles. Would Kearny come along? Hardtack wasn't exactly Kearny's favorite meal, but at that moment he was hungry enough to eat anything, and thirsty enough to drink from a mud puddle.

—Yes! said General Kearny. My orderly and I would be delighted to sup this evening with Sickles.

Gus had seen General Sickles on many occasions, during the past battles, bravely commanding a brigade in Hooker's division of the Third Corps.

Hooker showed Kearny the fancy invitation that Sickles had sent, and declared:

—This has got to be one of Sickles' jokes. You know he has nothing to eat but brown sugar and hardtack.

Upon arriving at Sickles' headquarters, the guests dismounted and Heintzelman said gruffly:

—None of your jokes, Sickles! What's the meaning of this fancy invitation for just some hardtack and brown sugar?

—Let's see, said General Sickles, bringing the group to a small grove of willow trees.

As they approached, the guests beheld a most wonderful sight: a snowy-white tablecloth spread out on the grass, covered with sparkling silverware, white napkins and porcelain plates filled with roasted chicken, baked ham, and fresh vegetables and fruits.

—Sickles has plundered a plantation! shouted General Kearny.

—Or he has robbed a hotel! added General Hooker.

Sickles grinned and as soon as the party was seated, two servants appeared with two large pails filled with purple colored liquid, garnished with loads of ice, fresh strawberries, sliced oranges, pineapples, and lemons. Kearny seized one pail and Hooker the other. Both dropped to their knees as if in adoration. Kearny then grasped a piece of ice and pressed it to his lips as if it were a diamond.

—Where did all this come from? asked Heintzelman.

Sickles gave an evasive answer that he had somehow deviously purloined the fine cuisine from a colonel in the Fifth Corps.

Later that evening, the general and his orderly rode leisurely back to camp.

—That was some feast, eh, Gustav? I expected the usual brown sugar and hardtack.

—Yes, sir! It was a feast fit for the Forty Thieves!

HEADQUARTERS IN THE FIELD.

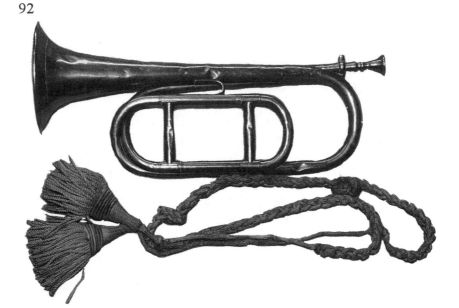

This bugle was given to Gustav Schurmann by General Phil Kearny at Harrison's Landing in July, 1862. It was manufactured by Klemm of Philadelphia.

The bugle call was vital on the field of battle for communication between command and operations during the Civil War. It was the only method of directing vast numbers of troops through complicated battle tactics. Since signals for both the Union and Confederate armies were identical, confusion often resulted as the two opposing sides drew closely in battle. Each unit had to know the particular sound and style of its bugler to properly identify the order. Without a doubt, each soldier of Kearny's division could easily recognize the playing style of Gustav Schurmann, making his position one of the most vital in the division.

The history of the bugle dates back to the ancient Hebrew shofar and to those animal horns blown in the armies of Gideon and Saul. Homer wrote of the bugle sounding in battle; his Greek countrymen held competitions in trumpeting in the Olympic games four hundred years before Christ. The limited scale of five open tones that can be played on a valveless bugle have not changed since the armies of Caesar.

Chapter Nine

In early August, General McClellan's failed Peninsula Campaign was abandoned. The Third Corps was ordered to return to Washington to join Major-General John Pope's army on campaign against Stonewall Jackson in Northern Virginia. Kearny's division left Harrison's Landing and began the long march back to Yorktown, where they were to board transports headed north. It was a difficult march because of the unmerciful August heat. The soldiers became tired, footsore and very hungry.

Kearny and his little bugler rode a few miles ahead of the division to examine the roads to Yorktown. Stopping at a farmhouse, Kearny was approached by a Rebel farmer who complained that the soldiers had stolen his chickens.

—I don't want to know anything about your damn chickens. I want to know where this road goes to, replied the general.

While the general and the farmer argued, Gus wished he could find himself a chicken to plunder. The thought of a delicious roasted chicken dinner made Gus's mouth water, but the whole area had been picked clean. Even the infamous Forty Thieves came up empty. A little further along the road, Gus spotted through the trees a farmer making preparations to bring in a fine flock of sheep he had hidden in the woods. General Kearny and Gus rode up to him and the general offered to buy one.

—I have none to sell, said the farmer.

—Yes, said Kearny, but there are crowds of hungry

soldiers just over the hill, and you had better sell out while you can. What will you take for the whole lot?

—Two hundred dollars, he replied.

Kearny paid the farmer in gold, and that evening the camp had delicious roasted mutton for supper.

On August 20th, Kearny's division finally arrived at Yorktown and began boarding steamers bound for Alexandria. Gus saw some shiny, brand-new soldiers guarding the steamers. These men had just enlisted and had come down from Boston the day before. Kearny's battle-hardened veterans teased them and laughingly called them "fresh fish." The new men all looked very dandy, dressed up in nice clean clothes with their shoes blacked, hair neatly trimmed, and wearing white gloves. They were a great contrast to the dirty, ragged and sunburnt veterans who had gone all through the bloody Peninsular Campaign. Gus laughed while some of the boys poked fun at the new recruits:

—Say, mister, what was the price of white gloves in Boston when you left?

—Don't they all look pretty? Be sure to keep the mud off them nice shoes!

—Any of you fellers want to buy a "trophy of war"? said one veteran displaying his bullet-riddled hat.

After arriving at Alexandria, the division traveled west by railroad to Catlett's Station and joined with Pope's army. Unfortunately, the supply wagons had been left behind, and the troops were in a destitute condition. Food and supplies were very scarce; many of the soldiers' shoes had worn out completely, and these men had to go barefoot. The soldiers were promised an issue of rations and new uniforms which were stored at the Union supply depot at Manassas Junction. Despite the poor conditions, they were full of spirit for a fight, and as General Kearny passed his soldiers on the road they cheered him enthusiastically.

On August 27th, Manassas Junction and all the much needed supplies intended for Pope's army were captured in a surprise raid by the Confederates under Stonewall Jackson. That night, after destroying the junction, Jackson did not wait to be attacked at Manassas, but withdrew to a position west of the old Bull Run battlefield. A confused General Pope ordered his scattered army to concentrate on Centreville, believing that Jackson had headed in that direction. The men of the Third Corps began their march to Centreville, thoroughly exhausted and very hungry.

Along the road to Centreville, Confederate cavalry harassed Kearny's division on all sides. Gus rode along with Generals Kearny and Birney, followed by a company of infantry. As they approached a wooded area near Blackburn's Ford, just south of Centreville, Kearny ordered Birney to cautiously advance his skirmishers. Suddenly, a mass of Rebel cavalry descended upon them. A cavalryman pointed his carbine at Kearny's chest and shouted at him: "You are my prisoner!" Kearny drew his pistol and retorted, "Am I?" and shot the Rebel dead. The rest of the Confederate cavalrymen turned and fled.

On the 28th, the sounds of war could be heard again with the boom of artillery off in the distance. It was about noon when Gus saw General Pope and staff arrive at Centreville. As he came into view, General Kearny rode down to meet General Pope and asked if he should put his regiments in advance towards the old Bull Run battlefield. Pope said, "No, I want General Burnside to get to a certain place before you start."

General Kearny was very indignant, and came back twitching his horse's rein impatiently. If Kearny had his way, he would have had a lively fight with the enemy that very afternoon, for as it was, the Confederate army had all day to get into a good position and be well prepared to meet the Union forces the following morning.

Early in the morning of August 29th, Kearny's division was on the move towards Jackson's position and everything seemed to indicate a fight. The Confederates were entrenched behind a railroad embankment in thick woods. All morning Pope's army tried in vain to get the Rebels out of those woods and now General Kearny would try his hand.

Division headquarters was located on a clear ridge, where Kearny gathered his brigade generals and several aides-de-camp, who at once became an inviting target for Confederate artillery. One of the enemy's batteries fired a projectile at the exposed group. The shell struck to their left, and Kearny laughingly said, "They are aiming at me again!" but it did no harm other than to scatter dirt and gravel all around.

As they rode, Kearny announced to his staff that he would personally lead the assault. The general pointed to the west and said, "Gentlemen, in one hour we will have that Rebel flank rolled up, or Phil Kearny loses his other arm."

The general had the occasion to write an order, which he did crouching on one knee, while Gus steadied the paper with his fingers. Noticing that Gus's hand was trembling some, Kearny asked him, "What's the matter?"

"Nothing," Gus hesitated, "only...I am a little frightened."

"Never get frightened!" Kearny said with the strongest conviction. "You must never get frightened at anything!"

Kearny was truly fearless. Gus believed that any person other than Kearny would have felt just the same as he did, for the way the Rebels were throwing shot and shell in that particular spot was a terrifying glimpse of what was to come.

The assault column was formed and Kearny, followed by his little bugler, rode alongside the column of troops encouraging them, "Come on my good boys, don't see me go alone into those woods! Damn them! Damn the Rebels!" He then drew his sword, clenching the reins of his horse between his teeth, and spurred his mount towards the Rebel line.

Gus raised the bugle to his lips, sounded the charge, and

followed his general. The clear, clarion notes echoed in the woods, and caused the brigade to "hurrah" and lurch forward at the double-quick. Gus noticed that some of the infantrymen brought their caps down over their eyes as if they were bracing against a strong wind.

The Confederates held their fire until Kearny's men had advanced within twenty paces. Then, a terrific sheet of flame and smoke burst forth from the Rebel line and the air became filled with flying lead. The front rank of blue disappeared from sight. Gus felt a minié ball whiz past his head so closely that it made his hair stand on end. It seemed to him a miracle that he was not hit as men were dropping all around.

The Federals smashed into the Rebel line, capturing many and bayoneting those who resisted. They soon fought their way to a railroad cut beyond the Confederate lines where they watched the enemy break for the rear.

It seemed that victory was at hand. However, Kearny's force had suffered considerable losses, and great numbers of Rebel reinforcements could be observed gathering in the distance. Kearny used Gus's back as a writing desk and dashed off a message requesting support. Gus trembled a bit, and Kearny shouted: "Damn it, boy! Keep still!" All through this vortex of hell, Gus clenched his bugle and struggled to keep by the general's side through the thick smoke and swirling mass of horses, flags and men. Kearny then handed the order to a lieutenant and said:

—Tell General Pope to hurry with supports, for we cannot hold out much longer!

Moments later, General Birney appeared through the thick smoke and shouted:

—General, the enemy is massing for a counterattack! I don't think we can hold this position without reinforcements!

—There are no supports, said Kearny bitterly. Turning to Gus he ordered the recall.

Gus sounded the call with his bugle, several times, with all of his might, for he knew that this call must be heard by all of the regiments in the brigade.

Thousands of howling Rebels began to descend on the decimated brigade. The bullets flew around them like hailstones. Kearny called to his bugler, "Let's get out of this...as quickly as God will let us." Gus put his spurs into Baby's flanks and she dashed into retreat. This was the first time Gus saw Kearny run from an enemy, but all knew it was sure death to stop.

When they emerged from the woods, the survivors of the brigade rallied and halted the Confederate counterattack. Sporadic firing continued until sunset when darkness ended the fighting for the day.

Later that night, a captured Confederate was brought into Kearny's headquarters for questioning. He was lean and dirty, about twenty-eight years old. His knees could be seen through the gaping holes in his gray trousers and his hair stuck out through the holes in his slouch hat. A guard seated the prisoner beside the campfire and gave him some hardtack. Gus watched as the prisoner devoured his food ravenously.

—Thank you kindly, the Rebel said, as Gus poured some hot coffee into a blackened tin cup. When the prisoner took a big healthy swig of the delicious liquid, his eyes grew wide and bright.

—Genuine Yankee coffee! the prisoner exclaimed. This is a rare treat. Thank you, and bless you, my boy!

Sizing up the little bugler, the Rebel continued:

—We have some young-uns in our army, just about your size too, and totin' muskets! My name is Allen C. Redwood, and I'm pleased to make your acquaintance.

Gus asked Redwood to which outfit he belonged.

—Fifty-fifth Virginia, he replied. I was gobbled up this afternoon. That was some fight today, wasn't it?

—Yes it was, indeed, said Gus. I never saw fighting so

desperate.

—Oh, yes, said the Rebel. Were you in many fights?

—Williamsburg, Seven Pines, all through the Peninsula with General Kearny, Gus said pointing to the red badge on his cap with pride.

—Yes indeed! said Redwood. You "red diamonds" are fightin' Yankees and your General Kearny is every inch a fighter, for sure. He is the one Yankee general that we fear and respect. It seems that our generals can whip any Yankee general anytime, time and time again, 'cept the "red diamonds!" I declare he must be protected by a hidden coat of armor. Our officers point him out to the men and say, "never mind the other Yankees, shoot at that one-armed devil!" and a hundred or more of our best marksmen aim their muskets at him and he always rides away unscathed. That, my boy, is a charmed life.

Gus felt pleased with the respect the Confederate had for his general. He then noticed that the prisoner was now looking very tired and began to shiver some.

—Take this; the night's getting cold, he said, handing the prisoner a blanket.

—Thank you, kindly, said Redwood. Tomorrow will be a hot one for sure. As you all know, Longstreet is up and Lee will begin to attack you. Best prepare yourselves for another Bull Run.

Reveille was not necessary the next morning, for the booming of cannon awakened Kearny's exhausted veterans. As the staff mounted their horses, an officer mentioned to Kearny that this day would decide the battle.

"No," Kearny shook his head. "Don't say so to anyone else, but the chance of success was thrown away yesterday. Had Pope supported my flank attack by a vigorous charge on the enemy's front, we would have overwhelmed Jackson's inferior force. It is too bad, for I lost many fine fellows in our attempt to gain ground we can now never recover."

The general and his little bugler rode outside the line of battle to scout the Confederate position. They had no sooner advanced beyond the line when the Rebel sharpshooters commenced making a target of them. Some of the men hollered at Kearny to return, but he took his time, until he saw all that he could see. Then he condescended to turn his horse's head and show the enemy his rear.

As Kearny and Gus emerged from the woods they came across a young woman, about sixteen years of age. Fresh blood covered her hands, and her apron looked rusty with dried blood. She was carrying bandages along with several canteens, giving water to the many wounded men scattered all around. General Kearny watched her for a moment then called out, "You there; what is your name?"

"Annie Etheridge, sir," came the reply. "I am a nurse in the Third Michigan Regiment."

"I am impressed by your bravery and the care you give to these poor wounded men so near the firing line," spoke General Kearny tenderly. "Anything you can do to ease the suffering of my wounded men touches my heart. You are a kind, and gentle soul. I will see to it that you receive a sergeant's rank and pay, along with a horse and any medical equipments that you may need."

"Thank you, General," said Annie. "Thank you very much."

From that moment on, she was forever known by the men of the division as "Gentle Annie."

By mid-afternoon, Generals Robert E. Lee and James Longstreet launched a massive attack against the undermanned Union left flank. The overwhelmed Federals were quickly routed and began to withdraw in wild disorder--just as they did the previous summer on the same battlefield. Kearny exploded in a fit of rage when he learned about the collapse of the left flank.

At about eight o'clock that night, just as the last light of day was vanishing, a dismal rain began to fall. Kearny, followed by his bugler, rode up to General John Gibbon the commander of the Iron Brigade which was positioned as rear guard.

"I suppose you appreciate the condition of affairs here, sir? It's another Bull Run, sir, it's another Bull Run!" Kearny said to General Gibbon.

"Oh, I hope it's not as bad as that, General," replied Gibbon.

"Perhaps not," said Kearny. "I am not stampeded, you are not stampeded. That's about all, sir, that's about all!"

The Battle of Second Bull Run was a defeat for the Union army, and during the night they solemnly retreated to Centreville. Early on the morning of August 31st, General Kearny secured a small cottage in the village to be used as his headquarters. The staff was kept busy all during the day scouting the surrounding countryside, and until late in the evening preparing their reports. At midnight Gus wrapped himself in an overcoat and fell asleep next to a warm fireplace.

Early the next morning, September 1st, General Kearny summoned Gus into his room.

—Yes, General? said Gus, approaching Kearny's bedside where he lay with papers spread out atop his blanket.

—Gustav, my lad, I have an important duty for you, he said, handing Gus a few official documents and a pass. Please take these letters, including this one to my wife, and have them posted in Alexandria.

Reaching over to the table by the bed, Kearny took three or four golden dollars and some silver.

—This will defray your expenses, said Kearny placing them into the bugler's hand.

In the dim lighting of the room, Gus could see lines of deep worry across the general's ashen face. Until this time, he had never thought of General Kearny as an "old" man; in fact, in many ways he seemed as youthful as a drummer boy. Perhaps the general was just tired. Then it struck Gus that his general looked just like his father during his illness. Before Gus could speak, Kearny said:

—Go, now, before daybreak. This will be a fearfully long day, and I will need you by the end of it.

—Yes, sir, Gus replied. Is there anything else I can do for you?

The general turned to Gus and partially smiled, a smile emanating mostly from his eyes, which gave Gus a measure of reassurance.

—Be sure to watch for Rebel cavalry! And return safely. Now go, quickly!

Gus left the cottage and stepped out into the chilly morning air. He buttoned his overcoat and wondered what lay in store that day. Gus climbed into the saddle and pointed Baby to the east, where purple and crimson clouds streaked the early morning sky. When the sun finally appeared on the horizon, it was blood-red.

A mile or so down the road heading towards Alexandria, Gus encountered a group of Union cavalry videttes who told him to go no further.

—The Rebels are attempting to cut off our army from Washington, warned a cavalry sergeant. This road is not secure.

Determined to carry out his orders, Gus took a detour south and arrived in Alexandria by late afternoon. He posted the general's letters along with one of his own and started on the return journey. The road was clogged with thousands of wounded and retreating men; it reminded Gus of the retreat from First Bull Run the previous summer.

As Gus rode on, he faced a strong wind blowing from the west and the sky was beginning to darken with angry clouds. He fixed his india-rubber blanket over his shoulders just as a violent thunderstorm broke overhead. Baby became hesitant and skittish at the continuous crashes of thunder.

—What on earth is wrong with you, Baby? Gus wondered. It's only heaven's artillery. He then put spurs to the nervous animal to encourage her forward.

Gus learned from some stragglers that Kearny's troops were engaged near Chantilly, a few miles west. In the darkness, Gus proceeded as far to the front as he dared, not knowing the Federals' position. He remained with Baby under a tree by the roadside all night, enduring the heaviest downpour he had ever been in.

By next morning, the rain had subsided and Gus was anxious to continue his ride back to the general. Spotting some soldiers wearing the "red badge," Gus inquired of the whereabouts of General Kearny's headquarters.

"Kearny's either dead or a prisoner," came the soldiers' reply.

Gus was dumbfounded. Kearny, dead? Never. This could not be.

—Where can I find General Birney? he stammered. His mind was racing. What could have happened? The anxiety was almost too much to bear.

Gus galloped to General Birney's headquarters and there he found out from the general all he could about the battle of the previous evening.

"At the time, it was raining," said General Birney, "and the smoke from the battle hung low. I galloped down to send a regiment to protect my left. Kearny accompanied me; as we leaped a ditch his horse shied and he remarked: 'How disagreeable to have a horse behave that way in battle!' Kearny then told me that he would reconnoiter a certain gap in the line which was left unguarded. I advised him not to go as the woods were filled with Confederates. Kearny, in his impulsive manner, said that he would go anyhow. He then galloped to the right and I saw no more of him. I returned to the battle expecting to find him; but he had not been seen. I presumed he was a prisoner and had the entire battlefield searched for him during the night.

Through the darkness and the blinding sheets of rain he rode straight into a Confederate skirmish line."

An exchanged Federal prisoner told the rest of the sad tale:

"The 49th Georgia regiment was lying in ambush as General Kearny rode up to within ten paces of them, when he suddenly brought his horse to check. The entire regiment rose to their feet, and leveled their pieces at him. They were clothed in Federal uniforms captured from our supplies at Manassas Junction. At this the general made the following characteristic interrogation:

'What regiment are you, God damn you?' to which they made no reply.

He again asked: 'What regiment are you?' To which they answered:

'Surrender yourself a prisoner!' Then the general shouted, 'Never' and, throwing himself down upon his horse's neck, dashed away. The Rebels opened fire and a minié ball struck Kearny in the spine. He was killed instantly. So ended the life of the warrior Phil Kearny."

After hearing the tale, Gus walked a short distance away, sat down on the ground, and wept. Despite his soldierly pride, the death of his hero unmanned him.

—The bravest man in the Army of the Potomac has fallen, Gus said to himself. God curse the villain who shot him.

In an admirable demonstration of military courtesy, Kearny's remains were returned to Union lines the following morning under a flag of truce, and then conveyed to Alexandria.

On September 3rd, Kearny's staff officers somberly escorted their general home to New Jersey. He was buried in old Trinity churchyard in New York City. Baby, as part of Kearny's personal property, was returned to the general's widow. Gus sadly parted with the horse, assured that she would provide some small consolation to the distraught family.

After the Battle of Chantilly, the Third Corps retired to the defenses of Washington. The command of Kearny's division now fell to General Birney, who retained Gus as division bugler. Birney's first order was to have all the men in the division keep the red diamond patch on their caps in memory of their late commander. General Kearny's life and death had bound the members of the *Red Diamond Division* together as closely as brothers.

"He was the best General in the army," wrote a correspondent from the *New York Times.* "His loss will never be made up; every man in the division adored him. Many a poor fellow was seen on the road, crying for his loss--and I, too, do not blush for my manhood, when I acknowledge that I shed tears."

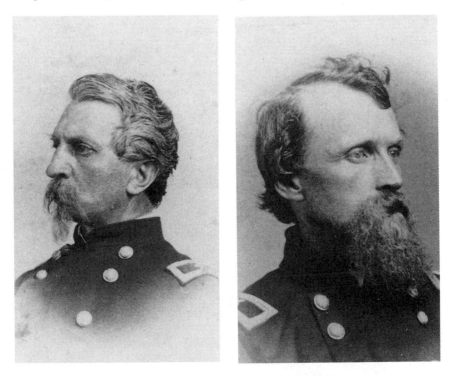

Gen. Phil Kearny (left), and Gen. David Bell Birney (right).

This photograph of Gustav Schurmann was taken by R.W. Addis in September, 1862. The type of image was called a *carte de visite*, which was an inexpensive paper print enabling Gus to have a dozen copies made for a dollar. General David B. Birney himself signed the bottom of the card: *"Gen. Birneys Bugler."*

Chapter Ten

After the Battle of Chantilly, there was a period of inactivity for the Third Corps. For several weeks Kearny's division encamped near Alexandria to recuperate from the exhausting Second Bull Run campaign, and to refill their depleted ranks. At this time, Lee's army invaded Maryland, and the rest of the Army of the Potomac pursued him, which culminated in the Battle of Antietam.

In mid-September, General Birney was ordered to report to the War Department in Washington and he requested that Gus accompany him. Gus was pleased to serve under his new commander. Brigadier-General David Bell Birney, age thirty-seven, was highly respected for his qualities as a man and his abilities as an officer, and he held the esteem and confidence of every man in the division.

While in Washington, General Birney stopped at a photographic studio on Pennsylvania Avenue to have his image taken. As the general sat for his portrait, Gus stood by and watched with keen interest and became fascinated by the long photographic process. When General Birney was finished, the photographer asked if Gus would like to have his image taken. Yes, by all means, insisted the general. It was the first time Gus ever had his picture taken and he wasn't exactly sure how to pose. The photographer made a few suggestions, and then went off to prepare another negative. After a little thought, the little bugler struck a soldierly pose--left hand on hip, right hand clasping his treasured bugle.

  —Yes, Gustav, that's it, grinned General Birney. You have

the swagger of a veteran!

When the photographer was finally ready, he instructed Gus to remain absolutely still, for the exposure would take several seconds. At last, Gus had a photograph of himself to send home to his beloved family. Several copies of the image were also presented to friends, and he even enclosed one within a tender letter of condolence to General Kearny's widow.

For the next several weeks, General Birney served on a court of inquiry, and Gus returned to division headquarters. In Birney's absence, Major-General George Stoneman was placed in command of the division. Stoneman was a cavalry officer commanding an infantry division. Although he was a stranger to Kearny's veterans, he soon came to earn their respect.

In early November, Gus received a wonderful gift from the officers of General Birney's staff with whom he had become somewhat of a favorite. They had presented him with a beautiful roan mustang that had been captured from a Rebel officer. Gus named his new horse "Pompey," and he and the filly spent hours racing across the golden autumn countryside.

Meanwhile in Washington, President Lincoln had become impatient with the inactivity of General McClellan and the failure to crush Lee's forces after the Battle of Antietam. The President relieved McClellan of command of the Army of the Potomac and replaced him with Major-General Ambrose Burnside.

On November 17th, General Birney returned to the head of the red diamond division, and General Stoneman was elevated to the command of the Third Corps. Gus remained with General Stoneman and was promoted to the distinguished position of corps bugler. Gus was proud of his new position, and wrote his parents a long letter to tell them of his prominent duty.

The Army of the Potomac began marching south towards its next objective: attacking Lee's army near the city of Fredericksburg. These plans quickly went awry, however, when rain began falling almost every day. Wagon trains that were miles in length clogged the muddy roads, making them impassable. This forced the infantry to laboriously slog through the fields. On November 19th, the Third Corps finally arrived near Falmouth, which was located on the opposite side of the Rappahannock River from Fredericksburg. The soldiers wondered what would happen next and after two weeks of inaction, some commenced building winter quarters.

The first week of December brought heavy snow storms and bone-chilling temperatures, and many soldiers became sick from exposure. Gus at least had a good tent over him, and was able to keep reasonably warm. At night, he looked out at the vast army, and reflected on the strange beauty of this encampment; the snow made the camp look more picturesque. The thick icy crust of snow sparkled in the bright moonlight like an ocean of diamond dust.

The Army of the Potomac was in close proximity to the Rebel army, with nothing separating them but the frigid waters of the Rappahannock River. Lee's army began fortifying the hills west of Fredericksburg, and soldiers on both sides were continually kept guessing as to what General Burnside really intended to do.

One afternoon, down by the river, Gus listened as Federal pickets conversed freely with the Rebel pickets on the other side.

—Got any tobacco?

—Yes.

—Give me some.

—Give me some coffee and I will.

—What do you have to eat?

—Hardtack and beans.

—When did you get paid last?

—So long ago that I can't remember.

—How do you like your officers?

—I don't.

—I say, Yank, what are we fighting about?

—I seem to have forgotten, Johnny.

—Well pard, let's throw our guns in the river and end this damned war.

One thing for sure, Gus realized, was that the entire war could be over in one afternoon if these pickets were left to settle it.

At dawn on December 11th, Gus watched as Federal engineers began constructing five pontoon bridges over the Rappahannock to Fredericksburg. When Rebel sharpshooters opened fire, the builders retreated for a short time. Federal artillery then shelled the city in an effort to drive the Rebels out, but the sharpshooters remained in position. Eventually, small detachments of Union infantry rowed boats across the river and after a tenacious defense the Confederates were driven out of Fredericksburg. A division of the Second Corps came up and successfully occupied the deserted city by nightfall.

Lee's Confederates strongly positioned themselves on the high ground west of the city, and spent the day of the 12th strengthening their lines. As night fell, it was obvious to all that Burnside was planning a major assault against the formidable Confederate position on Marye's Heights the following day.

Early in the morning of December 13th, Stoneman's Third Corps began crossing the river about three miles below Fredericksburg. Gus was posted at Third Corps Headquarters, within sight of the river, and was able to see the battle progress. At about noon, he witnessed the gallant charge upon Marye's Heights. Gus watched in awe as thousands of Federal troops advanced with muskets gleaming, bayonets flashing, and flags waving. Then, from the Confederate heights above, a circle of fire shot forth as a hundred cannon blasted gaping holes in the Union regiments. An immense cloud of fire and smoke rolled over the battlefield, and scores of boys in blue disappeared from Gus's view. The scene was an inferno, and even from his vantage point, the roar of battle was deafening. The attack did not last long--only about thirty minutes. When it was over, thousands of Federal soldiers lay dead and dying on the field. Never before did Gus witness such senseless slaughter.

Gus and Pompey kept close behind General Stoneman as the battle raged on. Then, a volley of Confederate artillery shells rained down on them. Though Gus was a bit shaken by the sudden explosions, he was pleased that Pompey behaved so well under this heavy fire and never even flinched.

General Stoneman and his staff rode through this storm of shot and shell to converse with General Daniel Sickles, commanding the Second Division. Suddenly, a bounding cannonball passed within inches of Gus's head and tore clear through the horse of a staff officer a few feet away. The animal let loose a piercing shriek and instantly fell dead. Sickles and Stoneman turned in their saddles to see the little bugler's reaction to such a close call. Both Gus and Pompey stood firm, like a statue. The bugler's only thoughts were of General Kearny's words: "Never get frightened! Never get frightened at anything." The Battle of Fredericksburg ended as another tragic defeat for the Army of the Potomac. More than 12,000 Federals were listed as killed, wounded, or missing.

On Monday night, December 15th, Burnside ordered the army to retire back across the Rappahannock. As the survivors of Birney's division trudged back to their old camps at Falmouth, Gus trotted Pompey alongside the long column. Gus thought the men looked more forlorn than he had ever seen them, and he began to worry for his country and his cause. Along the route, Gus passed some of his former comrades in the Mozart regiment. Though the regiment's losses were heavy, their spirits were not dampened. A little further along, Gus saw Sergeant Brady marching at the head of Company I.

—*Halloo*, sergeant! Gus saluted.

—*Halloo*, Gustav! God be praised!

Gus anxiously asked the sergeant how the regiment fared in the battle.

—We fought for three quarters of an hour, Brady replied, the enemy *peppering* us, and we *salting* them. As you can see, there isn't much of the regiment left--only about two hundred and fifty of us--which isn't many when you consider that another regiment has already been consolidated with us.

—Where are my mates in the drum corps? Gus asked.

—They are back assisting the surgeons, answered Brady. You must come visit us soon!

—I will as soon as I can, shouted Gus as he spurred his horse to catch up with General Stoneman.

As the bugler rode off, Sergeant Brady heard one of the new "consolidated" men sneer at Gus:

—When did they start letting little babies into the army? Go on, little baby, your Mamma's calling!

Sergeant Brady angrily eyed the obnoxious soldier and shouted:

—Quiet in the ranks, you fresh fish! That *little baby* was once considered too small and too young to be a drummer for the Mozart Regiment. Well, let me tell you, a braver or more loyal boy never lived! That little bugler rode alongside the one-armed devil himself and now trumpets for the gallant Third Corps--so shut yer hole!

Several weeks of inactivity passed until January 21, 1863, when General Burnside began another campaign to attack Lee. This second attempt involved crossing the Rappahannock south of Fredericksburg. This time, Burnside was defeated by the elements as a torrential rain storm continued for thirty hours, making the roads impassable. Wagons, caissons, pontoons, animals, and men were all stuck in the deep Virginia mud, and as a result the men dubbed the campaign: "Burnside's Mud March." The effort was called off, and the soldiers returned to their winter quarters at Falmouth doubting Burnside's brains and ability.

The mounted officer on the right is General George Stoneman, in front of his winter quarters under construction in January, 1863. Standing second from left is Gustav Schurmann.

General Daniel Sickles (above), Federal Corps Badges (below).

Chapter Eleven

On January 25, 1863, General Burnside was relieved of command and replaced with Major-General Joseph Hooker, who immediately began to reorganize the beaten army. General Stoneman left the Third Corps and was given command of the cavalry of the Army of the Potomac. Major-General Daniel Sickles was placed in command of the Third Corps and Gus was assigned to his headquarters as bugler and orderly. Sickles was forty-three-years old and had been a U.S. Congressman from New York before the war. He had gained notoriety for killing his wife's paramour, the son of Francis Scott Key.

General Birney's division still proudly wore Kearny's red diamond upon their caps. In his official report of the Battle of Fredericksburg, General Stoneman wrote: "Amongst the stragglers and skulkers the Kearny badge was in no one single instance observed."

General Hooker, realizing the value of Kearny's system, expanded it throughout the Army and a unique symbol for each Corps was chosen: the colors red, white, and blue were assigned respectively to the First, Second, and Third Divisions. The First Corps wore a sphere; Second Corps, a trefoil; Third Corps, a diamond; Fifth Corps, a Maltese Cross; Sixth Corps, a Greek Cross; Eleventh Corps, a crescent; and the Twelfth Corps wore a star.

After the debacle of Fredericksburg, officers of the Third Corps went to great lengths to improve morale among the rank and file. Throughout the remainder of winter all sorts of schemes were devised to relieve the monotony of dreary camp life. General Birney was at the forefront in leading these efforts.

On January 30, 1863, Birney arranged such sporting events as horse races, footraces, and sack races--activities similar to, but on a more extended scale than, those that celebrated St. Patrick's Day in the Irish brigade.

The horse races were the most exciting and were usually comprised of a hurdle race, steeple chase and a flat race. Dozens of officers entered their mounts and a large amount of money was wagered. Many elegant ladies in fancy dresses were invited down from Washington to watch the spectacle. Gus stood upon the grandstand with the generals and heralded each event with his bugle calls. Up and down the track in front of the stand a strong guard was drawn up, made up of the colorful Zouaves of the 114th Pennsylvania Infantry. As Gus surveyed the crowd, he spotted a woman soldier amongst the Zouaves, or, as they were known in the French army, a *Vivandière*. She wore a straw hat with a large plume, a yellow bodice, dark blue cloth jacket and skirt trimmed with red, a light blue sash, and scarlet trousers. Her name was Mary Tepe and she was perhaps the most well-known vivandière in the army. Armed with a revolver, she also carried a small keg of whiskey for the wounded or those who collapsed from fatigue on the march. She was always very kind to the sick and injured and would stay with the wounded until they were properly cared for. "French Mary" along with "Gentle Annie" Etheridge were highly regarded by the soldiers in the Third Corps.

The horse races finally began and Gus was thrilled by the spectacle. Several officers were thrown from their mounts during the races, resulting in a few broken bones. Next came the comical events in which the privates indulged: a footrace; climbing a greased pole; then a sack race. The spectators roared with laughter.

The camp festivities closed that evening with a concert

performed by Brigadier-General J.H. Hobart Ward's brigade band. Thus ended an enjoyable day that was long remembered by all those connected with the Third Corps.

In the first week of February, Gus received a letter from Agnes Kearny, the general's widow. She thanked him for his condolences and photograph, and mentioned a newspaper article about her late husband's role in the Battle of Second Bull Run which contained a reference to "Kearny's little bugler." Could that be him?

Mrs. Kearny wrote to General Birney expressing a wish to meet "the gallant little soldier," hoping to learn more details of her beloved husband's death. She asked if it would be possible for Gus to come to New Jersey. General Birney forwarded this request to General Sickles, who at once gave Gus a week's furlough. A telegram was sent to Mrs. Kearny confirming the arrangements.

Gus traveled by rail to Newark and was met at the station by a coachman in a fine carriage drawn by two handsome horses. It was a bitterly cold day and snow was beginning to fall. The carriage took Gus across the Passaic River to an impressive brick mansion high on a ridge east of the city. The elaborate edifice resembled a fairytale castle, he thought--a dwelling befitting the knightly Kearny.

The little bugler climbed the steps and entered the opened door of the mansion. A servant held a gilt candelabra aloft and bade him welcome. Gus's heart was pounding with nervous anticipation. He had never seen such elegance in all his life, and he was not certain what to say to the general's widow. The servant took his snowy cap and overcoat and informed him that Madame Kearny was waiting in the parlor.

Gus followed the servant through the great halls admiring the paintings with gilded frames and marble sculpture. He suddenly became aware of his jingling spurs echoing within the cavernous interior, and wished he had thought to remove them.

Gus stood in the doorway of the elaborately-furnished room with its magnificent crystal chandelier, carved ceiling, cornices, and elegant wallpaper. He marvelled at the heavy drapery, rich Oriental rug, and tables of black walnut. The room glowed with the warmth from the marble fireplace. Mrs. Kearny and her two young daughters sat upon a velvet settee.

—The general's bugler, announced the servant.

—Thank you, said Mrs. Kearny. Turning to Gus, she said graciously: Welcome to our home. Please sit down.

—Thank you; I am pleased to meet you, said Gus shyly, feeling out of place amidst such grandeur.

The widow wore a black mourning dress and Gus was struck by her youthful appearance. Agnes Kearny was a beautiful, auburn-haired woman with a delicate face and hands. As she introduced her daughters Susan and Virginia, Gus was reminded of his two baby sisters and began to feel a bit homesick.

—It is so nice of you to come visit us, and you have travelled such a long way, said Agnes. The children and I would like so much to hear of the final days of our beloved general, but first, you must be terribly hungry.

Indeed he was. Gus had eaten nothing since morning.

The four walked to the formal dining room where they sat on high backed chairs at a large mahogany table. The table was covered with a white embroidered cloth, and set with elegant china and silverware; this was a great contrast with the tin plate and cup that Gus had grown accustomed to in the past two years.

Gus watched the three place their napkins on their laps, and he did the same. A servant brought a pot of hot imported tea and a meal of broiled chicken, browned potatoes, fresh bread, cheese, lettuce, wafers, fancy cakes, and chocolates.

Gus had never eaten so well and so much. The hungry soldier impulsively used his fingers to seize a piece of chicken, then suddenly became aware of the others at the table watching him ravenously devour his meal; he remembered his manners and slowed down.

Mrs. Kearny smiled across the table at her hungry little guest and motioned to the servant to give him another helping of potatoes.

—You must please tell us how you were appointed the general's bugler, said Mrs. Kearny.

The story of Baby and the jump at Harrison's Landing delighted the widow and children. He concluded by saying:

"I believe my jumping that ditch brought me favorably to the general's notice."

Agnes Kearny smiled and the children's eyes were aglow.

"In battle," Gus added, "sometimes he used my back as a desk to scratch off dispatches, and he used to swear something awful if I trembled!"

—Yes, that sounds like my Phil, smiled Agnes. I am sure he saw in you the boy he once was. When he was about your age he was already known as a perfect daredevil on horseback, and his only dream in life was to become a soldier and serve his country.

Then Agnes Kearny's voice turned serious and grave:

"My heroic husband was sacrificed--sacrificed. The pang of sorrow is rendered more keen from the knowledge that he always felt he would be sacrificed in this war. He died a martyr in the Cause! My only regret is that our dear little Susan and Virginia are so young that in a few years they will have but a faint recollection of their father. He was a man worth remembering!"

Gus grew quiet. He felt great sympathy for the widow and her children. He gazed at the empty place at the head of the table and suddenly realized that this is where the general sat. The familiar song the soldiers sang in the evening by the campfire came to him:

We shall meet but we shall miss him,
There will be one vacant chair;
We shall linger to caress him
While we breathe our evening prayer.

Gus finally broke the long silence.

—In the past two years I have lost many friends and comrades while I have remained uninjured. The one I look back on with the most sadness is General Kearny. I looked up to him as the model of all that was soldierlike. For eight weeks I was constantly by his side, and sometimes I think that he knew death was near and so ordered me to Alexandria.

After a short pause, Gus continued,

"The general always treated me the same as my own father would have, and no soldier mourned his untimely death more than I did."

Mrs. Kearny then asked Gus about his own mother and father. Gus told her they lived in New York City and that his father had been discharged from the army due to illness. When she inquired how long it had been since he had last seen them, Gus replied it was nearly two years and though his family was in his thoughts constantly, his foremost duty as a soldier had cured him of any homesickness. Still he wrote home often and sent most of his pay, but the war had changed him and Gus wondered if his mother would see him as he saw himself now: no longer a boy, but a soldier who had witnessed the great struggle of life and death.

Upon hearing Gus's story, Mrs. Kearny insisted that he should return home the next day to visit his family, since New York City was only a short distance away.

—Your mother and father will be very happy to see you. You can't imagine what it's like for those at home when their loved ones are so far away. They wait eagerly for any word about their soldier and they dread the worst. Which battle did he fight in? Was he wounded? Or killed? Was the Union victorious? Or did we suffer another defeat? And when he is not fighting, they wonder if he is sick or well and always praying to God for his safe return.

Gus grew pensive. Perhaps in having been away from home so long he had forgotten how dear his family was to him. He realized that her words rang true.

That night as he settled down in the guest chamber he said a prayer for his mother, father, and sisters, and another for Mrs. Kearny and her daughters. Then Gus stared at the large feather pillows and the bright white sheets, realizing that it had been almost two years since he had slept in a bed. He thought of how many nights he had spent sleeping on the wet ground or, as the soldiers jokingly called it, "on the soft side of a hard board." He eagerly jumped in and pulled the covers to his chin. The warmth and comfort of the soft bed soon enveloped him and he quickly fell into a peaceful sleep.

The next morning after breakfast, Gus thanked the widow for her kindness and hospitality, and bade a fond farewell to the general's family. Mrs. Kearny handed Gus a letter addressed to General Birney, and once again thanked him for coming. Leaving the mansion, Gus walked through the snow to the stable where the coachman was preparing a sleigh to take Gus to the ferry at the Jersey City docks.

It was warm inside the stable and the smell of hay and horses reminded Gus of the army. In the far stall was Baby. The white horse bobbed her head and whipped her tail when she saw Gus. The mare seemed thrilled to see her old friend; she was a war-horse after all, and did not enjoy the dullness of pasture. Gus patted her nose.

—No riding today, girl. I'm going home.

Baby snorted and kicked her forefoot on the floor.

Bayard and some of the other horses also recognized the little bugler. Taking the cue from Baby, they stomped and snorted, anticipating the appearance of their slain master.

The coachman was amazed at the strange behavior of the horses. He stared in wonder as Gus related the stories of his adventures with these equine friends who had not forgotten him.

It was a long walk in the bitter New York City cold from the ferry to his old neighborhood. The city had not changed much since Gus had left, but the coating of fresh snow on the ground made the streets look cleaner and more picturesque. Gus reached his tenement and took a deep breath before he sprinted up the several flights of stairs to the Schurmann residence. He was glad to be back. It had been almost two years since he had left home-sweet-home!

Won't mother and father be surprised to see their soldier boy! he thought. Of course, mother will fuss, and yes, father will be so thrilled to hear of the exciting campaigns. Gus wondered if his sisters had grown much. He hadn't received any news from them for months.

As Gus reached the second landing, Mrs. Schwarz spotted the boy from the landing above and ran to tell the Schurmanns. Moments later, the front door of his home opened before he could even knock, and his two sisters ran out to greet him, nearly bowling Gus over.

—Mamma! Mamma! Gus is back! Gus is back! they shouted.

Suddenly, Caroline Schurmann appeared in the doorway wearing a simple black dress. Her eyes were red; she had been crying.

—Mamma, Gus said as he reached to hug her.

—Oh, my Gustav. My Gustav, she said, as she pressed him close to her.

Something was wrong. Gus sensed great sorrow as she touched him, and he felt a chill run through him.

—Come inside; come inside away from this cold.

Everything in the home looked the same as Gus had remembered, but there was a solemn stillness so quiet that the ticking clock on the wall sounded very loud to him.

Feeling uneasy, Gus asked for his father.

Dabbing her eyes with a handkerchief, his mother replied:

—Your father is dead, Gustav. Gone for nearly a week. Had you not received my letter?

Letter? Gus had not received any mail since Mrs. Kearny's correspondence.

—I wrote three weeks ago to tell you to come home, that Papa may not make it through another winter. Oh, it has been so cold, Gustav; so dreadfully cold.

Caroline explained that after Frederick's death she asked a neighbor's son--a cavalryman home on furlough--to return to the Third Corps headquarters in search of Gus. But by the time the trooper arrived, Gus had already departed for New Jersey.

The funeral had been a few days earlier with some friends and family in attendance, and Frederick was laid to rest in a cemetery in Brooklyn.

Gus sat beside his mother on the bed in shock. His sisters, who were too young to understand the meaning of death, looked upon the two with curiosity; at their tender ages they needed no real consolation. Gus wished he could be in their state of innocence again. But in the past two years, he had grown accustomed to death.

Embracing his tearful mother, Gus could shed no tears. He knew that he had to be strong for all of them. Of course his mother needed him at home now more than ever, but Gus made her realize that he had to fulfill the term of his enlistment. He spent the last days of his furlough making his family as comfortable as possible. Gus still had close to thirty dollars in pay which he used for food and coal for the stove. There was enough money to buy some material for dressmaking so his mother could supplement their meager income by sewing. Gus also visited his father's grave, now covered with a blanket of snow. He whispered a prayer for him, and another for his mother and sisters.

When the day arrived for Gus to return to the army, he told his mother not to worry; he would send home all his pay.

As he prepared to leave, his mother desperately clung to Gus and said:

—You promise to return to me, Gustav? You promise to be home next time for good?

What could he say? Life as a soldier had no certainties, no promises. Mother and son stood at the doorway and embraced.

—Don't worry, Mamma. I will be fine. Father always believed that God's blessing will be upon us. You must believe that too.

As Gus broke away and turned to go, his mother said:

—Wait, Gustav, you must take this. She pressed in his hand his father's beautiful silver pocket-watch. It played a soft, gentle melody when the case was opened.

—Your Papa wanted to give you this himself. He wanted you to keep this and remember that he is watching over you.

—Yes, Mamma, I will treasure it!

Descending the stairs, Gus finally felt the tears come to his eyes. He thought of the days before the war when his father had taught him to play the drum, and their months together as soldiers. He would never forget their last good-bye at the train station, nor any of the other times together. He hoped that his father was proudly watching over him now.

When Gus returned to camp on February 18th, he found the Third Corps blockaded in their tents by rain, mud, and snow. He immediately reported to General Sickles at headquarters.

The general and his staff, having just finished supper, were relaxing with cigars. Sickles summoned Gus to the head of the table where an aide produced a large box.

The general announced:

—Owing to your past gallant service and your advancement to the important position as bugler for the Third Corps, the headquarters staff believes you must now dress in a more befitting manner. We present you with this gift.

Inside the box was an elegantly-tailored musician's jacket made of fine blue cloth, piped with yellow. Gus noticed that the trousers had a sergeant's stripe down the leg. Such an honor, indeed!

—Thank you, sir! said Gus with great appreciation. He saluted the general, who mildly chuckled at the youth's enthusiasm.

—Congratulations, Sergeant Schurmann, said General Sickles as he shook Gus's hand.

—I only wish that my father could see this, Gus said regretfully, and told the officers of his father's death.

As the men expressed condolences, Gus remembered what his mother had told him about Frederick watching over him, and the sadness seemed to dissipate.

Leaving headquarters with his new uniform, Gus reached into his pocket and raised his father's watch to his ear. The soft melody brought him a sense of calmness. He was comforted by it, and felt his inner strength renewed.

Gustav Schurmann's jacket.

A 19th century charcoal portrait of Gustav Schurmann.

President Lincoln and his son Thomas or "Tad."

Chapter Twelve

In early April, 1863, the President, Mrs. Lincoln, and their ten-year-old son Thomas, also called "Tad," visited the Army of the Potomac. Reviews and inspections were held for several days, as the President had come to look over the troops and see what promise the men offered for the upcoming spring campaign.

A thrilling day unfolded for Gus on the morning of April 9th, when he began preparing for the Presidential inspection. Of course there were a great many things to do at headquarters; everything had to be cleaned and shined. Gus brushed his uniform, put on a clean collar and gave his boots a good blacking. At eleven o'clock President Lincoln and his family arrived with members of his cabinet and other dignitaries. The President's young son loved watching soldiers and seeing the soldiers' way of life. Nothing could have pleased little Tad more than to be at the army camp. At about noon, the gallant Third, Fifth, and Sixth Army Corps left their camps among the hills to assemble for the inspection on a wide, extended plain. Regiment after regiment and brigade after brigade came marching down from the surrounding hills with flags flying and bands playing martial music to stir the very blood. The well-disciplined troops marched in the bright sunlight singing the popular song:

We are coming, Father Abraham, three hundred thousand more,
From Mississippi's winding stream and from New England's shore;
We leave our plows and workshops, our wives and children dear,
With hearts too full for utterance, with but a silent tear;
We dare not look behind us, but steadfastly before,
We are coming, Father Abraham, three hundred thousand more!

On this occasion, as on all other occasions when visiting the army, Mr. Lincoln dressed in a long black frock coat and wore a tall silk hat, high top boots, and spurs. Though not a bad rider, he was anything but a handsome horseman in the midst of the gallant generals, colonels, majors, captains, and other officers who donned their impressive uniforms.

As General Sickles' orderly, Gus stayed close to him at all times and was able to get a good view of President Lincoln and his entourage.

"The President at the Review of the Army of the Potomac, April 9, 1863," is the title of this sketch by war artist Alfred R. Waud.

This detail of the Waud sketch is of special interest as the artist has depicted Gustav A. Schurmann riding behind the President.

The President rode on horseback from headquarters to the reviewing stand beside General Hooker with Hooker's staff and corps commanders trailing behind them.   As they rode along, President Lincoln took notice of the little boy orderly who rode alongside General Sickles.

"Who is that child?" asked the President.

"Oh, that's Gus; Kearny's little bugler," answered Hooker.

"This boy," spoke General Sickles, "is a great fighter. He was nearly killed while at Stoneman's side. Besides, he rode with Kearny and you know what that means."

When Tad first saw Gus, he could not believe his eyes, for Gus was someone close to his own age who was already what Tad longed to be: a soldier! Tad looked on as Gus rode about the field until Tad could stand it no longer and persuaded a cavalryman to lend him his horse.   The President's son approached the little orderly with the hope of befriending him.

—Hello, said Tad sheepishly. May I ride along with you?

Gus looked at General Sickles for approval.   The general nodded and said:

—Look after young Master Lincoln.

The two boys rode off at a canter. In comparison to Gus, Tad was not much of a rider and his short legs stuck straight out from the saddle. The boys bounded around the field with Tad leading the way and Gus following closely behind. More than once Gus helped the inexperienced rider stay in the saddle and not cause injury to himself. The two boys rode before the President's procession with Tad shouting to the soldiers at the top of his small voice, "Make way, men! Make way, men! Father's a-coming! Father's a-coming!"

The artillery broke forth with a thundering salute that echoed throughout the hills and set the air quaking about their ears. As the President and his escort cantered down the long line, regimental standards drooped in greeting and bands and drum corps, one after another, struck up "Hail to the Chief" until it played simultaneously in a grand chorus that made the hills ring.

Tad was a lively boy that day. He tuckered out his horse riding him up and down and into every camp. He had his nose into everything as he investigated every artillery park, provision train, cavalry camp, and infantry line. The soldiers would salute him as they passed and he would doff his cap in return. The soldiers, of course, made much of the friendly-spirited lad and gave him three cheers.

Tad expressed a consuming desire to see some live Rebels, or "graybacks" as he called them, so Gus escorted the President's son down to the Rappahannock River to a Union picket-post opposite Fredericksburg to have a look. Across the river, two Rebel pickets were warming themselves by a fire. Both of them wore Federal light-blue army overcoats. Noticing the boys' arrival, the sentinels playfully called out in mock alarm. Tad stood on a large rock watching the enemy pickets through a spyglass when a Confederate officer came down to the riverbank to investigate the shouting. The officer spotted the two boys, took off his hat and made a sweeping bow, and walked away. Tad announced he was satisfied with his inspection of the enemy's position, and the two boys hurried back to the review.

At the end of the long day, the President and Mrs. Lincoln were preparing for their return to Washington. They called for Tad, bidding him to take leave of his new playmate.

"Mother, I won't go home unless Gus can come along too."

"Oh, no," said the President, "that won't do. This lad is a soldier, and must remain here and attend to his duties."

"I don't care, Pop. I want him to come home with me and teach me to ride and blow the bugle."

This earnest appeal and the tears filling Tad's eyes overwhelmed the tender heart of the President.

To relieve the Commander-in-Chief from embarrassment, General Sickles said, "Mr. President, if you desire, the bugler may accompany you. I will give him a two-week furlough."

Tad was overjoyed and thanked the general. Gus hurried to his tent to secure his knapsack, hardly believing his good fortune. He was actually going to be a guest in the White House! Gus joined the President and his family at Aquia Creek Landing, and traveled by steamboat to Washington that night. The next morning, he rode to the White House in the Presidential carriage.

As the carriage passed through the large iron gate, Gus stared at the impressive mansion and wondered aloud:

—Oh, if only father was here to see this.

—Has your father passed on, my child? asked Mrs. Lincoln.

—Yes, Ma'am. He died two months ago. We both enlisted together in '61, but he soon took sick and was discharged.

—You poor child, said Mrs. Lincoln. So many are suffering in this cruel and unnatural war. Then, turning to her husband, she said: "Don't you think it's a shame to have such children in the army?"

Tad and Gus kept up a racket until late that night when Mrs. Lincoln told them the President was tired and needed rest. As Mrs. Lincoln opened the door of the chamber where the President slept, Gus saw the head of Abe Lincoln peeking out from under a long white nightcap. Alongside the President's bed, there was a trundle bed in which Tad slept. Mrs. Lincoln showed Gus to the guest chamber down the hall. The room was even more impressive than his accommodations in the Kearny mansion. That night, Gus slept serenely. When he awakened the next morning, he rubbed his eyes and wondered if it all wasn't a dream.

Shortly after sunrise, a loud knock on the door was followed by Tad bounding into the room shouting with glee:

—Good morning, Gus! Rise and shine! It's time for my bugle lesson, but first I want to show you my new pony!

Tad had just received a pony for his birthday and was anxious to ride him. Gus quickly donned his uniform, pulled on his boots and the two boys ran down to the stables.

Gus was given a beautiful mare to ride while Tad saddled his new chestnut pony.

The two boys climbed into their saddles and off they went at a furious pace. After exhausting the horses, the boys stopped to rest. Tad was eager for his first bugle lesson, but after a few attempts they both realized he did not have an ear for music, nor strong enough lungs to play such long and complicated calls. Tad gave it up, satisfied with his one lesson from the little bugler.

Later that afternoon, Mrs. Lincoln introduced Tad to his new tutor. Tad took one look at the bespectacled man holding an armful of books and bolted away, shouting that it was time for another bugle lesson. Tad later told Gus that tutors came and went at the White House like changes of the moon. None stayed long enough to learn much about him and his rambunctious ways. Tad always did his best to avoid learning his lessons.

"Let him run, Mary," said the President to Mrs. Lincoln. "There's time enough yet for him to learn his letters and get pokey."

Gus thought Tad was a generous-hearted, sweet-tempered lad but soon learned he had an adventurous and mischievous mind. On Sunday afternoon, when a storm kept the two boys indoors, Tad's budding genius took a particularly destructive turn. Fetching a small hatchet, said to be the one that little George Washington used to chop down the cherry tree, Tad planned a similar scheme. He hacked at various pieces of furniture and finally sawed away the banisters of the main stairway. When servants reported this activity to the President, Tad and Gus were immediately summoned to Mr. Lincoln's office.

Though he had been a witness and not a participant in this vandalism, Gus was petrified and dreaded the worst. He imagined Tad might say: I cannot tell a lie, Pop; Gus did it!

Would he return to General Sickles in disgrace? Would he be discharged from the army? He wondered if the President would say that he was the worst guest ever at the White House.

As the two boys entered the office, the President politely asked them to be seated. Then, with an air of genuine hospitality, Mr. Lincoln entertained the boys with a story about the Black Hawk War, and showed them the sword he carried in that campaign as captain of a company of volunteers. Never once did he allude to the act of vandalism.

Later that afternoon, Tad was burdened with a question for his father, but the President was busy at an important meeting of state. Tad, followed by Gus, went to the Executive Office door and loudly rapped three times in quick succession, followed by two slow raps. He then burst into the office like a thunderbolt, ran up to his father, and embraced him. Gus noticed that Secretary of War Edwin M. Stanton and Secretary of State William Seward were in the office and seemed annoyed by the disturbance. Father and son spoke for only a brief moment and then Tad loudly ran from the room. Gus saluted the President and Cabinet members, and left.

"Mr. Lincoln," exclaimed Secretary Seward, "are you not annoyed by those boys?"

"Oh, never mind," smiled the President. "It's a diversion, and we need diversion in the White House."

One day, when another April shower kept the two boys indoors, Tad took the opportunity to show Gus his impressive collection of toy soldiers. The collection was a boy's dream. Gus stared in awe at the beautifully-carved, hand-painted armies of infantry, cavalry and artillery scattered about the room. Gus reached down and picked up a meticulously detailed Zouave infantryman.

—Oh, sighed Gus, how I wished for just one of these soldiers as a Christmas present when I was a young boy.

As Gus looked upon the painted face of the little toy Zouave, he recalled vividly the corpse of the dead Zouave he stood over at Seven Pines. The wooden figure somewhat resembled the countenance of the dead man.

Gus placed the toy back on the floor and realized he no longer had any desire to play with toys.

Tad sensed his new playmate seemed bothered, and questioned him:

—What is it like to be in a battle? I think that it must be thrilling! Have you ever been frightened?

—Yes, I have been frightened, and I have trembled in my boots. A battle is not at all like you see in the picture-books; no one is frightened in the picture-books. The most frightening time in battle is when artillery fire comes down around you. The few seconds between the bursting of a shell above and the striking of the fragments on the ground is the most frightening moment I know. First you hear the explosion--not as loud as the cannon but a hard dull noise; then come the fragments. There is no use in dodging for no one knows where they will strike. The thing is soon decided with a BANG, RATTLE, CRASH, and SLUCK! The slucking sound is the fragment entering some poor soldier. And then you look around and see one or maybe a dozen men rolling on the ground headless, armless or legless....

Gus paused, and continued:

—I once thought that war was thrilling, but no longer. I have been in eight battles so far, and have never received a scratch. God's will, I guess.

Tad gazed out the window. It had stopped raining and the sun peeked through the clouds.

—Don't worry, Gus. Pa believes that it's all in God's hands and Providence watches over us all. Let's not talk about the war anymore. Let's go outside for a ride.

Gus and Tad owned Washington for a fortnight, doing pretty much as they pleased. Tad was very fond of the theater and the two boys attended several plays. On the night of April 18th, the pair went to see a play at Grover's Theater called *The Marble Heart*, in which the leading role was played by a dark, handsome man with brilliant eyes. This was the actor's first performance in Washington, and the poster outside the theater announced:

THE PRIDE OF THE AMERICAN PEOPLE,
THE YOUNGEST TRAGEDIAN IN THE WORLD!
A STAR OF THE FIRST MAGNITUDE!

The two boys were enthralled as they watched the drama. The dashing actor with his great personal magnetism and raw energy kept the boys spellbound with his performance. At the end of the first act, Gus and Tad looked up the actor's name in the program.

"I'd like to meet that actor," said Tad. "He makes you thrill."

Immediately after the second act, the two boys went backstage and were led to the dressing room of John Wilkes Booth.

"Mr. Booth," said the stage manager, "this is President Lincoln's son." The actor shook each boy's hand and flashed a captivating smile. Continuing to apply his make-up, Booth asked the boys how they liked the play and the two told him which parts they most enjoyed.

When the stage manager announced the third act, Booth then rose and dramatically threw a black cloak over his shoulders.

—Perhaps, one day, your father will come and watch me perform.*

Tad nodded and as the boys prepared to leave, Booth handed each a rose from a bunch that had been presented to him over the footlights. The boys thanked the handsome actor and returned to their seats for the rest of the unforgettable performance.

*Abraham Lincoln saw Booth in *The Marble Heart* in November, 1863.

John Wilkes Booth

Tad Lincoln on horseback in March, 1865.

All too quickly, Gus's two-week furlough ended. Tad made Gus promise he would come visit again soon, and the two boys shook on it. Gus thanked the President and Mrs. Lincoln for their generous hospitality. As a parting gift, Mrs. Lincoln then presented Gus with a book of history. Tad liked this idea so much that he immediately ran to his room, picked up several of his lesson books from the floor, and gave them to his friend.

The little bugler returned to Third Corps Headquarters on April 23rd, and reported for duty to General Sickles. The general received him kindly, and inquired about the boy's stay at the White House. He then showed Gus a copy of the *New York Herald*, dated April 11, 1863. In it was a detailed description of the President's review, with a mention of the budding friendship of Gus and Tad:

...Master Lincoln, with his characteristic enterprise, booted and spurred, rode bravely at the side of the President, followed by a dashing little orderly. And hereby hangs a tale. When the war broke out a smooth faced lad came down with the troops and with them went into the fights. General Kearny noticed him and made him his bugler, and all through the struggles on the Peninsula kept him at the front of the division. Kearny fell but the bugler remained and, under the new commander, thrived as before. Now he trumpets for General Sickles at the head of the corps, and sports his sword belt and broad sergeant's stripes with the air of a veteran. A favorite among the officers his lot is far from being commiserated, while his future cannot but seem promising. Some have already been taken for giving him an education, and an appointment to the military school is hinted by his friends. Yesterday he accompanied Master Lincoln as inseparably as his shadow, and after the review initiated him into the science of managing the lance. The boys are fast friends, and ramble around together like brothers. Will their future histories be ever connected?

Gus beamed with pride and grinned ear to ear.

—*The New York Herald!* he exclaimed. A military education! West Point! His mind raced and his hopes soared.

—After we whip Bobby Lee in the next fight, said the general, this war will be over and we will surely have to start thinking about your future.

He informed Gus that a new campaign would soon be underway, and there was much work to do in preparation.

142

The following article appeared in the *Evening Star*:

FROM THE ARMY OF THE POTOMAC.

REVIEWS BY THE PRESIDENT.

THE ARMY IN SUPERB FIGHTING CONDI-
TION.

[Special Correspondence of The Star.]
Headquarters Army of the Potomac,
April 9, 1863.

Editor Star: The grand review, on the 8th instant, by the President, of four of the army corps of the Army of the Potomac—the 2d corps, commanded by Major General Couch; the 3d corps, commanded by Major General Daniel E. Sickles; the 5th corps, commanded by Major General Meade; the 6th corps, by Major General Sedgwick—was a magnificent spectacle. The officers and men never presented a finer appearance, more soldierly bearing, or were ever in better spirits or better fighting trim.

Among the finest troops present was the corps of Major General Sickles, which was in splendid condition, and showed that they were in a high state of discipline.

Tommy Lincoln, with his companion, Gustave Albert Schuman, (not yet fourteen years old, and who was with General Kearney through all his battles except the last one,) were both mounted on fine horses and attracted considerable attention. The President intends sending his son to West Point Academy, I hear.

Mrs. Lincoln, Mrs. Major General Stoneman, Mrs. General Carr, Mrs. General Graham, Mrs. Colonel Farnam, Princess Salm Salm, Mrs. Gen. Griffin, (daughter of Judge Carroll, of Washington,) and several other ladies, were present.

The mud is drying up fast, and the men are "spiling for a fight"

At noon to-day the President will review the 1st, 7th and 9th army corps, and will probably not return to Washington until to-morrow.

Chapter Thirteen

The position of the two armies had not changed since the Battle of Fredericksburg. General Hooker conceived a plan which he believed would finally crush Lee's army. A portion of the Army of the Potomac was left to confront the Confederates at Fredericksburg, while the rest of Hooker's army marched rapidly to the north and successfully crossed the Rappahannock River, placing them in the rear of the Confederate army at Chancellorsville. Then Hooker surprised everyone by taking a defensive posture. He had given up the initiative and Robert E. Lee took the opportunity and went on the offensive. Lee left a small portion of his army at Fredericksburg to confront the Federals there, and sent Stonewall Jackson's corps to attack the unprotected right flank of the Army of the Potomac.

On the morning of Saturday, May 2nd, Gus was stationed at Third Corps headquarters located along a plank road not far from the Chancellor family mansion, also known as Chancellorsville. Union pickets spotted a Confederate wagon train rapidly heading south and reported this to headquarters. General Sickles, believing it was a Confederate retreat, ordered General Birney's division to advance about one mile ahead of the main line and attack. Birney's movement appeared to be successful and hundreds of Rebels were captured.

A few hours after Birney's attack, Gus heard terrific firing from the Federal right wing where the Eleventh Corps, commanded by General Oliver O. Howard, was positioned. The Confederates Sickles had seen had not been retreating, but maneuvering around to attack the unprotected Union right flank. The captured Confederates had only been a rear guard.

Jackson surprised Howard's corps and stampeded them, which cut off Birney's division from the rest of the army. Howard attempted to rally his shattered corps, but his efforts were futile. His men were so panic-stricken that no power on earth could stop their running from the attacking Confederates.

On a ridge about two hundred yards away, Gus watched as 10,000 Confederate soldiers poured deadly volleys into Howard's men. The Federal artillery was in disarray; only a few guns were properly manned. Wagons, ambulances, horses, men, cannon, and caissons were all jumbled together in one inextricable mass.

Gus had never seen so much confusion and panic. General Sickles quickly assessed the situation and prevented the rout from affecting the rest of the army. He told Gus to stay close and keep his bugle at the ready. He dispatched each member of his staff, lest any should fail, in the attempt to warn General Birney of the danger and order him to fall back. Sickles and the little bugler then rode to the center of the mass of confused men and rallied them.

As night fell, General Birney's division was still separated from the main army and was slowly being encircled by the Confederates. Birney gathered his brigade commanders and announced in a low tone: "Gentlemen, the plank road must be retaken before daylight."

General Birney devised a plan and prepared his division for a midnight bayonet charge to cut through the Rebel lines surrounding them. At about nine o'clock that night double columns were formed, and at ten the signal was given to advance. The Red Diamond Division fought their way by moonlight through enemy lines and returned to the plank road. It was during the confusion of this night action that Stonewall Jackson was accidentally shot from his horse and mortally wounded by his own men. Kearny's veterans were pleased by this, considering it a fair exchange for the death of their beloved general.

That night Gus was unable to sleep. He spent the long night lying on the ground wrapped in his overcoat, holding his horse's lead in his hands. The scattered gunfire kept him awake and very restless.

Just before daybreak, a tap from General Sickles announced reveille. As usual, it was hardtack and coffee for breakfast in the saddle. While Gus munched his hard-cracker, an officer from Hooker's headquarters arrived with an order for Sickles, who was surrounded by his staff. Just as the group pressed in toward the messenger, a shell came screaming from over a distant hill and landed in a large mud puddle nearby. Some mounted officers leaned forward in their saddles and galloped hastily away, others threw themselves flat on their faces into the mud. Fortunately the shell did not explode, and although Gus was uninjured, he and his breakfast were completely bespattered with mud, water, and dirt.

—Dammit! he shouted. I'll make the Rebels pay for that!

General Sickles had a hearty laugh at Gus and the muddy breakfast, and then continued with the business at hand.

Sickles dispatched a staff officer to request reinforcements from General Hooker, whose headquarters were at the Chancellor mansion. Shortly after the aide left, the general summoned Gus and sent him to Hooker's headquarters with an additional message. Gus spurred his mount and rode off quickly. In a short while he reached army headquarters and handed the message to one of Hooker's staff officers. Enemy artillery shells were flying all around them. General Hooker stood on the front porch of the house, leaning against a giant pillar, when a Confederate cannonball dropped the column on him, rendering him senseless for the rest of the day. As the battle raged on, Hooker was in a daze, half-conscious and not fit to command an army in battle.

With more than 17,000 casualties, the Battle of Chancellorsville was yet another defeat for the Army of the Potomac. The beaten army withdrew across the Rappahannock to its former camp near Falmouth.

But for all the disappointment brought on by the Battle of Chancellorsville, this battle was not a blunder and a disaster like the one fought at Fredericksburg. The Army of the Potomac was not discouraged and demoralized as it had been during the past January, and was soon ready in body and spirit to fight the Rebels again.

At Falmouth one night, General Sickles sent Gus to deliver some official documents to Colonel Egan of the 40th New York. Gus was glad for the opportunity to visit his old comrades in the Mozart Regiment. After delivering the order, Gus emerged from the colonel's tent and bumped right into his old sergeant. A surprised Sergeant Brady loudly laughed, and placed his big hands on the bugler's shoulders.

—Gustav! Welcome home, my lad!

Then noticing the sergeant's stripe on the bugler's trousers, Brady corrected himself.

—Pardon me, welcome home, Sergeant Schurmann! You're a sight for sore eyes.

The two soldiers laughed and shook hands. They had not seen each other since Fredericksburg. As they walked down the company street and talked about recent news, Gus mentioned the sad passing of Frederick. While Brady expressed his sympathy, Gus could not help but notice that the camp seemed somewhat empty. The ranks of the Mozart Regiment were thinning; so many familiar faces were gone. A few paces away, the bright glow of a campfire illuminated the scene.

—Is this the lair of the Forty Thieves? Gus inquired loudly.

His comrades exploded with cheers and greetings when they saw their old friend.

—Hello, pard! shouted Tommy Connolly. Make way for the general's puppy!

Gus laughed and shook hands all around, then sat down by the fire.

—Hey pard, have you heard the news? laughed Tommy. Glass-Put-In has put down his drum and is now shouldering a musket!

Glass-Put-In smiled and nodded his head.

—Yes, this is true. I want to see my share of fighting on the firing line, and besides, the regiment needs rifles.

—He is right, Gustav, said Brady. We have lost over eight hundred men since Williamsburg, and we need to fill up our ranks.

—Just keep your glasses on and aim low, advised Tommy, and you should come out safe and sound.

Glass-Put-In's expression then turned serious:

—I trust that the Almighty has kept me safe thus far, although much danger may be before me. If it is God's will that I find my grave in the South, let it come when it may. I am determined to do my duty.

Tommy then softly sang:

> *If amid the din of battle,*
> *Nobly you should fall,*
> *Far away from those who love you,*
> *None to hear your call.*
> *Who would whisper words of comfort,*
> *Who would soothe your pain?*
> *Ah! the many cruel fancies*
> *Ever in my brain.*
> *Weeping sad and lonely, Hopes and fears, how vain.*
> *When this cruel war is over, Praying that we meet again.*

Off in the distance the regimental bugler began to play Taps.

As the mournful notes echoed through the camp, the men grew quiet. The Army of the Potomac was preparing to sleep. Gus bid his friends goodnight, and started back to headquarters. Along the way, he thought about the many friends and comrades now gone, and prayed that he would be permitted to see the dawn of peace. Although memories of his deceased comrades saddened him, his devotion to the preservation of the Union was still unwavering.

Several weeks later, General Birney devised a plan to honor the memory of Phil Kearny by issuing an award to those who performed gallantly at Chancellorsville. This medal, known as the "Kearny Cross of Honor," was presented to five hundred selected men of the Red Diamond Division in recognition of their bravery and good conduct as soldiers. The selection process was difficult; so many individuals had distinguished themselves on so many bloody battlefields.

On the afternoon of May 27th the entire First Division was assembled. The men were required to be in their best attire, with shoes blackened and arms well-burnished. The sun shone brightly and a few clouds dotted the beautiful blue sky. At two o'clock, the troops, accompanied by their bands of music, marched to the parade ground. The band of the Third Brigade led the way playing *The Battle Hymn of the Republic*. The battle-torn flags of the sixteen regiments in the division fluttered and snapped in the breeze. Gus and Pompey followed closely behind Sickles and Birney, by the side of the division color bearer. The adjutant shouted:

Form square. Right and left into line, wheel. MARCH!

Gus sounded the call, and the other buglers echoed the command. General Birney's order was read by the adjutant:

"The Brigadier-General commanding the division announces the following names of meritorious and distinguished non-commissioned officers and privates, selected for their gallantry as recipients of the 'Kearny Cross,' the division decoration. Many deserving soldiers may have escaped the notice of their commanding officers, but, in the selection after the next battle, they will doubtless receive this honorable distinction."

At the request of General Birney, General Sickles presented the medals. Each meritorious soldier's name was called out, and the honoree was presented with a neat package containing a medal and a copy of the order. The recipients were then positioned in the center of the square, arranged in order by their respective brigades and regiments.

When the names of Mary Tepe and Annie Etheridge were called, the men of the division gave three cheers, and the two women blushed with pride. Immediately following, Gus was astonished to hear his name also being called as a recipient of the Cross. Generals Sickles and Birney each had broad grins on their faces and Gus blushed too at this great honor. As he dismounted and walked to the center of the square, the men in the ranks shouted:

Another three cheers for the little bugler!
Hip! Hip! Hurrah!
Hip! Hip! Hurrah!
Hip! Hip! Hurrah!

It was the proudest moment in his young life.

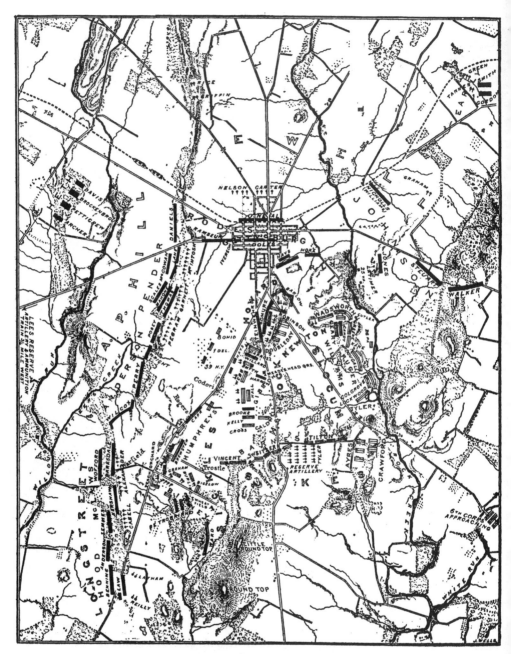

Troop positions at 3 P.M. on July 2nd.

Chapter Fourteen

After the Confederate victory at Chancellorsville, Robert E. Lee began maneuvering his army in preparation for an invasion of the North. The war was beginning its third summer, and the weary eyes of both nations turned to the small Pennsylvania town of Gettysburg.

During a period of inactivity for the Army of the Potomac in early June 1863, General Sickles received a request from Tad Lincoln asking him to grant Gus a second furlough to visit the White House. Of course the general would accommodate the President's son. The enterprising Tad had a surprise planned. With great excitement and anticipation, Gus hurried to Washington wondering what his rambunctious friend had in store for him this time.

At the White House, Gus was not disappointed. Tad announced that he was going to put on a play for the benefit of the Soldiers' Hospital, with the price of admission fixed at ten cents. Gus would have an important role playing the bugle.

Two days later, after several rehearsals, Tad's benefit performance was held on a small stage set up in one of the White House's larger rooms. The audience was chiefly comprised of soldiers, government officials, and a few society ladies. The President entered the hall looking deeply concerned, but brightened at the sight of Tad's little stage. Gus thought of the President's words, "we need diversion in the White House," and this play was certainly a diversion.

Before the curtain could rise, a courier arrived and handed the

President a message that General Lee's army had just invaded Pennsylvania! This meant that the Confederate army now threatened Washington, Baltimore and even Philadelphia! The audience sat in stunned silence for a moment, and then all was confusion. Gus watched the face of the President turn grave.

Mr. Lincoln quietly asked Tad to please raise the curtain and begin his play, for there was certainly a lot of work before them.

Tad's play had only one performance.

Gus's furlough was cut short, and the next morning he started for Third Corps headquarters with General Sickles, who also had been on leave. En route to the army encampment at Frederick, Maryland, they learned that General Hooker had been relieved from command of the Army of the Potomac and replaced by Major-General George G. Meade. There was an unsettled feeling among the men in the ranks, as they had no knowledge of General Meade's capabilities, and they feared yet another defeat. Many believed that a Confederate victory on Northern soil would mean the end of the Union.

On the march through Maryland, Gus heard some of the men talking about General Meade and the impending battle, when one eloquent soldier jumped up on a stump and said:

Soldiers of the Army of the Potomac; take out your little books; I am neither a prophet, nor the son of a prophet, nevertheless, I am about to prophesy, so draw pencils, ready! aim! The traitor army of Northern Virginia, in the trackless forests of Virginia, surrounded on all sides by traitorous Virginians, and commanded by arch traitors Lee and Jackson of Virginia, *is one thing*. But Lee and his army, without Jackson, on open Northern soil, surrounded by loyal men, women and children of the North, *is another thing*. The next battle is on the free soil of old Pennsylvania, and Lee is whipped, no matter who commands us; do you hear me? Shoulder pencils. Parade is dismissed.

The soldiers laughed and gave the fellow three cheers, and Gus became convinced that the next battle would decide the outcome of the war.

On Tuesday, June 30th, the Third Corps marched cautiously towards the Pennsylvania border, knowing only that the Confederate army was somewhere to the north and west. The Federals were now in loyal country which had not been ravaged by the war, and the citizens cheered them as they passed, presenting them with flowers, fresh bread, and cakes.

While riding through Emmitsburg, a pretty Maryland girl, just about Gus's age, approached him with a small bouquet. As he leaned down from his saddle to receive the fragrant present, the girl grasped his hand and kissed it.

—I am a Union girl, she said with a smile.

Gus blushed at the sentiment and thanked her. He would have preferred to stop, but the march could not halt for personal sentimentality.

—Good luck to you! she said.

Gus tipped his cap to her and rode on.

—Well, Gustav, smiled General Sickles, that little girl ought to bring you good fortune.

Later that day, Sickles and his staff made their headquarters in a farmhouse a few miles south of the Pennsylvania border just east of Emmitsburg, Maryland, while the Third Corps bivouacked in the nearby fields.

During the afternoon of Wednesday, July 1st, General Sickles received a message from General Howard, informing him of the fighting near Gettysburg, and that General John Fulton Reynolds, commander of the First Corps, had been killed. The situation was desperate, and Sickles was asked to bring up the Third Corps without delay. The general and his staff left Emmitsburg immediately and rode towards Gettysburg, arriving at the

Evergreen Cemetery's gatehouse by evening. The remainder of the Third Corps arrived just after dark. The Rebels were jubilant over the first day's fighting, and with the results so encouraging, Lee planned to attack again the next day.

In the early hours of July 2nd, Sickles surveyed his position and decided he was uncomfortable on the low ground north of a rocky hill called Little Round Top. Sickles feared Rebel artillery units would gain the ridge along Emmitsburg Road, thereby enabling them to enfilade the entire Union line. After pointing this out to General Henry J. Hunt, commander of the Federal Artillery, Sickles chose to move his entire corps forward to occupy the Emmitsburg Road.

General Sickles nodded to Gus who sounded the advance with his bugle, which was then echoed by the division and brigade buglers. Gus thought it was a grand sight to witness this little corps of two divisions, about 10,000 men, gallantly advancing. The soldiers in the ranks were aware that this move meant a fight, and that their numbers were too few to cover so much ground.

Birney's left flank was positioned at a mass of giant boulders called Devil's Den, and the line continued across a wheatfield, over a stoney hill into a peach orchard, then turned north along the Emmitsburg Road. General Andrew Humphrey's Second Division continued north along the Emmitsburg Road, facing west. General Sickles made his headquarters at the center of the line near a farmhouse owned by the Trostle family.

Great numbers of Rebel infantry were spotted in a wooded area a half-mile to the west of the road, causing Sickles to believe the Rebels were trying to pass around his left flank. He sent an aide to General Meade's headquarters asking Meade to come and examine the new position, but Meade, who was busy elsewhere, could not come. Shortly afterwards, General Meade summoned Sickles to his headquarters, but by the time they reached Meade's headquarters, the growing sound of musketry from Birney's front could clearly be heard. The meeting between the two generals was very brief. General Meade assured Sickles he would meet with him later on the field. Soon after General Sickles returned to the peach orchard, 15,000 of General Longstreet's veterans commenced a series of attacks against the Third Corps. Union artillery was brought into line and began firing at the enemy crossing the Emmitsburg Road to outflank the Third Corps' left.

General Meade, followed by his staff, arrived and called out: "General Sickles, I am afraid you are too far out."

"I will withdraw if you wish, sir," replied Sickles.

"I think it is too late," said General Meade. "The enemy will not allow you. If you need more artillery, call on the reserve."

Just as Meade finished speaking, a shell exploded nearby and frightened General Meade's horse into an uncontrollable frenzy. The horse reared and galloped away with the general, and Gus saw no more of the commander of the Army of the Potomac. From that moment on the air was literally filled with bullets, cannonballs and all sorts of exploding artillery shells. The fighting was of the most desperate character. The entire line of the Red Diamond Division was threatened, but Kearny's veterans were not easily driven from their position.

The thin line swayed to and fro throughout the fight, and regiments were moved repeatedly from one part of the line to the other to reinforce assailed points. General Ward's brigade in Devil's Den was in danger of being overwhelmed, and in dire need of reinforcement. The Mozart Regiment, positioned near the wheatfield, was sent to Ward's aid. Colonel Egan gallantly led the regiment in a bayonet charge down what became known as the Valley of Death, giving Ward the necessary time to fall back. In the wheatfield, Colonel Régis de Trobriand's brigade fought desperately until they were out-flanked and compelled to withdraw. Meanwhile, General Charles K. Graham's brigade in the peach orchard was bracing for an attack.

As the battle raged all around him, General Sickles sat calmly on his horse near the farmhouse, directing staff officers to bring up supports to the threatened line. At about six o'clock, brigades from the Second and Fifth Corps came up, counter-attacked, and temporarily halted the Rebel advance. Within minutes, however, the enemy regrouped and attacked again, all the while hollering their fiendish Rebel yell.

The enemy's artillery shells continued to fall near General Sickles and his orderlies, prompting them to begin a move to the rear of the farmhouse. As they turned their horses and started, a cannonball bounced past and struck the general below the right knee, breaking his leg nearly in two, but strangely causing no injury to the horse. Sickles dismounted, and called for Gus to bring something to bind the wound which was now bleeding profusely. Gus tied his handkerchief tightly around the shattered right leg, while an officer rushed to procure a saddle strap as a stronger tourniquet. Another orderly was sent to find an ambulance and surgeon.

At that very moment, the Union line broke in the Peach Orchard, and Federal infantry and artillery retreated past Sickles, with the Rebels in hot pursuit. Many of the retreating soldiers thought Sickles to be mortally wounded.

Sickles, seeking to reassure his troops, said, "No, no, not so bad as that, I am all right and will be with you again in a short time. You must hold your position and win this battle. Don't waver, stand firm, and you will surely win."

Minutes seemed like hours as they awaited the ambulance and surgeon. Gus anxiously watched over the wounded general as he lay there, growing more and more pale from loss of blood.

"If I die, let me die on the field," he muttered.

Just as a stretcher and ambulance arrived for Sickles, General Birney rode up and saw his critically wounded superior lying on the ground. Sickles called out: "General Birney, you will take command of the corps, sir!"

Quickly mounting Pompey, Gus was not sure if he should follow General Birney or stay with General Sickles. Then, just before he galloped off, Birney turned to Gus and said, "Go with General Sickles, my boy."

As he trotted alongside the ambulance, Gus saw Sickles smoking a cigar peacefully as the battle raged all around him--as if nothing unusual was happening. The wounded general was taken a half-mile to the rear to a farmhouse being used as the Third Corps hospital. Gus remained with the general until the surgeon arrived.

Meanwhile, reinforcements from the Second, Fifth and Sixth Corps arrived and halted the Rebel advance. Darkness soon brought an end to the fighting of July 2nd.

That evening, the surgeons amputated Sickles' mangled leg by the dim light of candles burning in the sockets of bayonets. The delirious general asked that his amputated limb be wrapped in a blanket and preserved as he wished to keep it as a special souvenir.

That night in the field hospital, surrounded by the dead and dying, was one of the darkest of the war for Gus. Throughout the afternoon and evening nearly 3,000 wounded men had been brought there. Now, in the sultry darkness of night, lit only by candles and starlight, Gus began a search for wounded Mozarters. He stooped and peered into the faces of the wounded, one after another, but it was too dark for him to determine identities in that way, so he began to ask each one the name of his regiment. The first was a member of the 3rd Michigan; the second, a corporal of the 17th Maine; the third, a Pennsylvanian; the fourth made no answer, though his eyes were wide open. Gus placed his hand on the man's forehead and felt the chill of death.

Behind a barn Gus found dozens of wounded Mozarters lying on the ground, and he quickly went to work securing food and water for them. A few paces away, he heard someone call out:

—Gustav! Over here.

Gus saw Sergeant Brady lying on the ground with a bullet wound in his thigh. Though suffering intense pain, the sergeant's eyes brightened when he saw the little bugler. Gus made a comfortable bed for the sergeant with some straw and an old blanket.

—Thank you, Gustav, and thank God you are well! So many are gone.

The wounded soldiers were disturbed by the awful possibility of another Confederate victory. Sergeant Brady told Gus of the Mozarters' gallant charge through the Valley of Death where he had been shot, then began to recount the long list of casualties. On hearing the names of so many comrades, Gus shook in anger.

The wounded sergeant grimaced, and said:

—I am willing to suffer all my pain if the Rebels are defeated. Our cause cannot stand another defeat.

—Lee will attack us again tomorrow for sure, spoke another wounded Mozarter. If they are victorious, our cause is lost.

On hearing this, Gus said coldly:

—Let the Rebels come tomorrow, and we will thrash them back to Virginia! They will forever regret entering Pennsylvania *and* leaving the Union! We will win this battle and this war.

The wounded sergeant smiled and admired the boy's spirit.

At daybreak on July 3rd, the surgeons decided that General Sickles' survival depended on removing him to Washington as soon as possible, and advised his staff to make the necessary preparations. Gus would go along as a mounted orderly.

The general, lying on a bloody stretcher, left Gettysburg with a force of forty stretcher bearers. He was to be carried to the nearest railroad point, where it was hoped he could be brought to Baltimore, then transported to Washington. As his pain was so intense, they progressed slowly. Sickles continually asked that cold water be poured on his burning stump, and Gus was kept busy refilling canteens in nearby streams.

By mid-afternoon, Gus heard the cannons at Gettysburg booming, and knew the battle was raging to a climax. All of the men fretted and worried about the fate of the Army of the Potomac and the Union. They had carried the general only four miles; with evening drawing near, they halted at a nearby farmhouse for the night.

Early next morning, as Sickles' entourage prepared to continue the journey, a courier riding from Gettysburg was stopped and asked the outcome of the battle.

—It is our greatest victory, he beamed. Lee attacked our center and was soundly defeated! Thousands of Rebels were captured! It is our greatest victory!

—Thank God! said General Sickles. Our country is saved!

Sickles arrived in Washington on Sunday morning, July 5th, and was brought to a private dwelling on F Street. He was placed in a room on the first floor, still lying on the same stretcher that carried him off the battlefield three days before. The surgeons were fearful that the general's wound would bleed anew, so they instructed that he not be moved from the stretcher.

Gus was outdoors when President Lincoln and Tad rode up to the front gate at about three o'clock. Having learned of Sickles' arrival, they had immediately rode there on horseback to call on him.

Gus entered the general's room to announce the President, and the two men shook hands cordially. Tad was respectfully quiet and also shook the recumbent general's hand. President Lincoln then sat down and questioned the general about the battle. He inquired about General Sickles' ghastly wound: how it happened, and how he was feeling. He sadly mentioned reports of the great casualties at Gettysburg and inquired about the care given.

All the while, General Sickles lay on his stretcher leisurely puffing on a cigar and answering the President in detail.

Occasionally he would wince with pain and call for Gus to wet his stump with cool water. When Mr. Lincoln's inquiries seemed to have ended, General Sickles puffed his cigar in silence, then introduced an inquiry of his own.

"Well, Mr. President, I beg pardon, but what were your thoughts while we were campaigning and fighting up there at Gettysburg? We heard that you Washington folks were a good deal excited, and you certainly had good cause to be. For it was 'nip and tuck' with us a good deal of the time!"

"Yes, I know that," said the President. "And I suppose some of us were a little rattled. Indeed, some of the Cabinet talked of Washington's being captured, and ordered a gunboat or two here, and even wanted me to leave Washington, but I refused to leave. I said, 'No, gentlemen, we are all right and we are going to win at Gettysburg;' and we did, right handsomely. No, General Sickles, I had no fears of Gettysburg!"

"Why not, Mr. President? How is that? Pretty much everybody down here, we heard, was more or less panicky."

"Yes, I expect, and a good many more than will own up now. But actually, General Sickles, I had no fears of Gettysburg, and if you really want to know I will tell you why. The fact is, in the very pinch of the campaign there, I went to my room one day and got down on my knees, and prayed Almighty God for victory at Gettysburg. I told Him that this was His country, and the war was His war, but that we really couldn't stand another Fredericksburg or Chancellorsville. And then and there I made a solemn vow with my Maker, that if He would stand by you boys at Gettysburg, I would stand by Him. And after thus wrestling with the Almighty in prayer, I don't know how it was, and it is not for me to explain, but, somehow or other, a sweet comfort crept into my soul, that God Almighty had taken the whole business there into His own hands, and we were bound to win at Gettysburg! And He *did* stand by you boys at Gettysburg, and now I will *stand by Him*."

At the end of the hour-long visit, the President and Tad said good-bye to the general and Gus and left.

In the weeks that followed, the weather in Washington became oppressively hot. The surgeons advised General Sickles to recuperate at Saratoga Springs, as the cooler air would accelerate the healing process. The general was given a pair of crutches to aid him in moving about, but he was having a difficult time with them. Gus would sometimes have to support the general's arm to keep him from falling.

On July 22nd, before they started for New York, Gus accompanied the general on a visit to the White House. As they waited outside the President's office, General Sickles told Gus he had asked the President for a favor regarding his future duty. The bugler was a little puzzled, but before he could question the general, a secretary told them the President was ready to see them.

As they entered the President's office, Mr. Lincoln stood up and greeted them cordially. After an exchange of pleasantries, the President turned to Gus, smiled, and said:

—Sergeant Schurmann, General Sickles and I have discussed your next assignment. Though it is true the Third Corps can hardly spare your services, it is your duty now, my boy, to return to New York and go to school and prepare yourself for West Point, for you have my promise to send you there.

General Sickles then spoke up:

—Your quick action in applying the tourniquet to my leg saved my life, and it would please me very much to thank you in this way. I have made all of the necessary arrangements for you to enter preparatory school next month in New York City. You will remain on my staff as orderly, but on "special duty," until your enlistment has run out.

—Thank you, general, and thank you, Mr. President! Gus

beamed. I believe I have only done what my father had taught me; my whole duty.

President Lincoln shook the little bugler's hand and said:

—You have done your whole duty very nobly, my boy, and you have the thanks of your country. You are a gallant little bugler and you will make a fine cadet.

Gus thanked the two men again and as he prepared to leave the office, Tad bounded into the room.

—Hello, Gus! the boy shouted. Secretary Stanton has commissioned me a lieutenant!

—Congratulations, Lieutenant Lincoln! saluted Gus.

—Is Pa going to send you to West Point? asked Tad.

—Yes, but not before I am prepared. I am sure that I will have to learn my lessons first.

Lieutenant Tad Lincoln

Chapter Fifteen

When Gus finally arrived home, Caroline Schurmann was overjoyed that her cherished son had returned from the war safely. She baked his favorite breads and pies, believing that he was much too thin, and continued to fuss over him. Gus was indeed happy to be home again with his mother and sisters. At times he would glance at his father's chair and miss Frederick greatly.

In the autumn of 1863, Gus entered school to continue his education in preparation for West Point, but he did not find academics to be easy. He had no schooling since 1860, and as a result had to be exceptionally diligent in his studies. Gus drove himself hard as a student, just as he did as a soldier.

Gus's favorite pastime was reading newspaper accounts of the campaigns of his former comrades-in-arms in the Third Corps. With feverish excitement, he poured over thrilling descriptions of the engagements of the Wilderness, Spottsylvania, Cold Harbor, and Petersburg. Then his elation turned to gloom when he read the names of friends who were listed among the killed, wounded or missing: General Birney died suddenly of malarial fever in October, 1864, while in the command of the Tenth Corps; Glass-Put-In (Private Willard Howe) was severely wounded at the Wilderness; and Colonel Egan was wounded leading a charge at Petersburg and later promoted to Major-General. Gus's old pard, Tommy Connolly, survived the war without a scratch. He came home with the survivors of the regiment in July 1864, and he and Gus resumed their friendship. Tommy eventually married and settled in Brooklyn.

Gustav Schurmann was discharged from the Mozart Regiment

on June 26, 1864. He continued his schooling through the spring of 1865, when the joyful news was announced that General Lee had surrendered at Appomattox Court House on Palm Sunday, April 9th. The war had finally come to an end.

Five days later the country's joy turned to sorrow. On Good Friday, President Lincoln was assassinated by the actor John Wilkes Booth, whom Gus and Tad had seen perform two years earlier. Booth shot the President in a theater box during a performance of *Our American Cousin* at Ford's Theater in Washington. The very moment that the President was assassinated, Tad was watching the play *Aladdin!, or the Wonderful Lamp* at Grover's Theater. The theater manager interrupted the play by walking out on stage to inform the audience that the President of the United States had just been shot. Someone in the audience shouted that it was a hoax; a ruse for pickpockets! Then a boy shrieked "like a wounded deer," said the newspapers, and ran from the theater.

Gus attended the President's funeral when the procession came through New York City, and it was the most solemn event he had ever witnessed. More than 150,000 people stood in line to view the President's body lying in state in the rotunda of City Hall. The building was completely draped in black cloth with the words "THE NATION MOURNS" placed over the entrance. Gus pinned to his coat a small black mourning ribbon which held a tintype likeness of the President, and stood in City Hall Park for hours awaiting his turn to view the fallen President.

The funeral of Abraham Lincoln at City Hall in New York City, on April 24, 1865.

President Lincoln's body in New York's City Hall.

While waiting in the long line, Gus thought of how little the park had changed since 1861 when he carried a shoe-shine box through it as a twelve-year-old boot-black. The park was the same, but the world had changed. *His* world had changed. Gus opened his pocket-watch and the soft melody brought a flood of memories to mind. His thoughts drifted from one blood-stained battlefield to the next, and he realized that the innocent child who wanted to be a drummer boy no longer existed. He had been hardened by war's horrors.

As Gus slowly approached the President's open casket and gazed down upon the well-known features for the last time, he shed tears for all the losses in his young life: his father, General Kearny, General Birney, scores of friends and comrades, as well as President Lincoln. Most of the people who had shown him kindness were now dead. Why did so many have to die? Gus then felt a calmness and peace--a "sweet comfort" entered his soul. He remembered President Lincoln's words just after the Battle of Gettysburg; how he had prayed to God for victory at Gettysburg. And for the past four years, Abraham Lincoln had borne the strife and suffering of the Country upon his shoulders. He had done his whole duty, nobly, and now God had called upon Abraham Lincoln to join Him in heaven.

—Rest in Peace, Father Abraham, said Gus quietly.

Gus never saw Tad Lincoln again. Some weeks after the funeral, Mrs. Lincoln and Tad went home to Illinois and in 1868 sailed for Europe so Tad could attend school in Germany. Gus often thought of his old friend and wondered if he ever learned to enjoy his studies. One day, Gus read in a newspaper that Tad returned to the United States, prostrate with a severe illness. He suffered for several months, then died on July 15, 1871, at the age of eighteen.

Gus had to forego the remainder of his own education when Caroline Schurmann became gravely ill in 1867, which required him to leave school and work to support her.

"President Lincoln's untimely death blew my prospects to the wind," Gus wrote to a friend in 1868. "My only hope of going to West Point is the election of General Grant as President, which General Sickles promised me."

GUSTAVE A. SCHURMAN.

Mr. Schurman was born in Prussia in 1849, but came here with his father when an infant. At the age of twelve years he joined the 40th New-York Mozart, in 1861, and was known as General Phil Kearny's bugler. He was in the battles of Williamsburg, Fair Oaks, the Seven Days' retreat, etc. At the battle of Gettysburg he was General Sickles's orderly, and was near him when the General received the wound that made necessary the amputation of the leg. Mr. Schurman is a bookbinder by trade. He never took a prominent part in politics until 1889. At the Republican State Convention in Saratoga that year, when the O'Brien faction was beaten, he was chosen to head the regular organization in the district, a position he has held ever since.

Sickles never did secure an appointment to West Point for his bugler. Despite the disappointment, Gus remained positive, believing he had already received a sufficient education and had experienced enough soldiering to last a lifetime. Gus became a bookbinder and later, through the benevolence of some former comrades, secured employment as a custom's agent in New York.

Gus kept in touch with many of his wartime friends over the years, sharing with them events such as his marriage to Anastasia Quinlin on March 6, 1870 (Tommy Connolly was best man), and the birth of their daughter, Lillian, on October 16, 1871. For many years, the family lived on Allen Street in Manhattan, and later at 100 East 104th Street.

Gustav Schurmann eventually became active in local politics, serving as president of the Republican Party of New York City from 1889-1892. He was also a member of the H.B. Claflin Post of the Grand Army of the Republic (G.A.R.) and Secretary of the Mozart Veterans Association. A newspaper account of a G.A.R. reunion in 1891 reported that, "the cheers never rose so wildly as when Gus Schurmann entered the hall and somebody got to telling about his fighting days with Kearny."

In July of 1888, Gus revisited the battlefield of Gettysburg during the Twenty-fifth Anniversary Reunion of the Blue & Gray. A ceremony dedicating the 40th New York monument was attended by thirty-six Mozarters and their families near the huge boulders of Devil's Den.

A patriotic song was sung, speeches were given, and a prayer was offered to the memory of those who had died. A photograph was taken of the survivors gathered around their memorial. Gus saw "Gentle Annie" Etheridge there, still proudly wearing her "Kearny Cross." The tattered and blood-stained flags were unfurled and saluted by the veterans with pride and reverence.

Veterans of the Mozart Regiment gather around their monument at Gettysburg. Standing second from right is Gustav Schurmann; standing fifth from right is Annie Etheridge.

After the ceremony, Gus walked for several hours touring the battlefield, revisiting such places as Little Round Top, the Wheatfield, the Peach Orchard, and the Trostle farmhouse. A remarkable contrast existed between these two visits--1863 and 1888. Now all was quiet and peaceful. The fields were broad and green; the air was filled with the sound of chirping birds.

Walking around to the east side of the farmhouse, Gus was surprised to see the old Third Corps battle flag hanging where it flew twenty-five years before. The yard was filled with hundreds of older veterans, some wearing gray, some wearing blue. Several of the men asked Gus if he was the son of a veteran--not thinking he was old enough to be a veteran himself. Gus simply replied that his father had been a soldier in the late war, and he was there only to honor the memory of those who had fallen. Moments later, a carriage drove up with Generals Longstreet and Sickles, sitting side by side, chatting as pleasantly and friendly as if they were brothers. They were immediately surrounded by a crowd of veterans, all anxious to shake hands with the distinguished generals.

Gus silently watched the scene from a distance, then continued his walk, very much satisfied that he had done his duty, his whole duty, and the nation was one again.

Gustav Schurmann died of tuberculosis on July 19, 1905, at the age of fifty-six. His wife Anastasia had died two months previous on May 11th. Their daughter, Lillian, died in 1958. They are all buried in the Schurmann family plot in Woodlawn Cemetery, the Bronx, New York.

The following obituary appeared in the *New York Times*:

WAS TAD LINCOLN'S CHUM.

Schurman Enlisted as a Drummer Boy When Eleven Years Old.

Gustave A. Schurman, who served as a drummer boy and bugler in the civil war, died on Tuesday at the home of his daughter, Mrs. W F. Wassman, 108 East One Hundred and Fourth Street, of consumption. He was fifty-five years old and had been ill about three years.

He served under Gens. Birney, Stoneman, and Sickles. He was but eleven years old when the war began, and was a bootblack in New York City.

The boy bugler attracted the attention of Lincoln in one instance, when the President, Mrs. Lincoln, and their son "Tad" were visiting the armies. "Tad" became interested in the boy in uniform, who was only two years older than he, and soon made friends with him. In one instance Schurman was said to have saved "Tad's" life in a runaway.

However that may be, Lincoln invited the young bugler to go to the White House with them, and the two boys often played there together.

Since the war Mr. Schurman had held positions in the Custom House and various city departments. His wife died several months ago. A daughter survives him.

GLOSSARY

adjutant--A staff officer assisting the commanding officer.

aide-de-camp--An officer on a general's staff.

battery--A unit of artillery consisting of four to six cannon or sometimes simply called guns.

brigade--Three to six regiments usually constituted a Union brigade.

caisson--A two-wheel cart or wagon with large chests for carrying artillery ammunition.

campaign--A series of operations in a particular theater of war.

canister--A tin can containing numerous iron or lead balls that scatter when fired from a cannon.

carte-de-visite--An inexpensive paper print photograph mounted on a small card.

cartridge box--A leather box worn on the hip containing rifle ammunition.

column--A formation of marching troops.

corps--Usually made up of two or more divisions.

division--Usually made up of three or more brigades.

double-quick--A trotting pace.

dress parade--A formal review of troops in their best uniforms.

earthworks--Trenches dug by the soldiers for protection from the enemy's fire.

flank--The right or left end of a military formation.

furlough--A leave of absence.

Grand Army of the Republic--The G.A.R. was the largest Union veteran organization after the war.

Grand Review--A parade or inspection of the entire army.

gum blanket--See india-rubber blanket.

hardtack--A durable cracker, made of flour and water and normally about four inches square.

haversack--A bag with strap worn over the right shoulder to the left hip.

india-rubber blanket--A waterproof blanket, treated with rubber.

light marching order--To travel "light," usually without knapsacks in order to be less encumbered for fast movement.

long roll--The drum roll command to assemble.

Minié ball--The standard bullet used during the Civil War. It was invented by Claude-Étienne Minié, a French army officer.

orderly--A soldier assigned to a superior officer for various duties, such as carrying dispatches or orders.

picket--A soldier placed as a lookout at a distant outpost.

pontoon bridge--Small boats anchored by beams followed by a series of tightly fitting planks to form a temporary bridge, in which infantry, cavalry and artillery can easily cross an unfordable river.

rammer--An artillerist's tool used to ram the projectile down the barrel.

shirker--A coward or someone who avoids duty.

skirmishers--Soldiers sent in advance of the main body of troops to scout out or probe the enemy's position.

sponge-staff--An artillerist's tool used to clear a cannon barrel of smoldering embers and grime between firings.

sutler--A merchant with a permit to remain with troops in camp or in the field who sells food, drink, and luxuries to the soldiers.

tattoo--The command to extinguish lights and prepare for bed.

vidette--A mounted scout.

vivandière--A woman who carried provisions to sell to the soldiers.

Zouaves--Regiments modeled after the original Zouaves of French Colonial Africa who wore colorful uniforms; usually red baggy trousers, short open jackets, and a turban or fez.

Acknowledgments

I would like to thank the following friends and colleagues whose unselfish assistance and continual support helped me tell the story of *The Little Bugler.*

Very special thanks goes to: Daralee Ota, Jim Nevins, Jack Fitzpatrick, Buddy Kruk, Sarah Willis-Blazejewski, Victoria Lopes, Bill Mapes, Pete Doroshenko, Tom Neely, Gary Kross, Bill Dekker, Rachel Simon, Cathy Pehlman, Henry Deeks, Rob Hodge, Jim Stevens, Carol Curren, Brian Pohanka, Dan Jones, Larry W. Ditch, Mark Lee, John Valori, Thomas C. Duclos and Bill Julien at the Division of Military & Naval Affairs, State of New York; Daniel Lorello at the New York State Archives; Scott Hartwig at Gettysburg National Military Park; Mike Maoney at Ford's Theater NHS; Mike Winey and Randy Hackenburg at the Military History Institute at Carlisle Barracks; May Stone and Mariam Touba of the New York Historical Society; Thomas Burke at the New York Public Library; the New York Hall of Records; the Museum of the City of New York; my mother Agnes Styple, and brothers Bud, Ken, Rob, and of course, my wife Nancy.

Picture Credits

The sources for the photographs are listed below:

On pages 13, 14, 22, 28, 32, 54, 76, 113, 128, 165, 166: MOLLUS Collection at the U.S.A.M.H.I., Carlisle Barracks. Page 39 (top photo): Larry W. Ditch; (bottom photo MOLLUS). Pages 25, 92, 126, 127: courtesy of The Division of Military & Naval Affairs, State of New York. All other photographs are from the collection of the Author.

Bibliography

The following books, newspapers, magazines, and special collections were utilized by the author:

Books

Billings, John. *Hardtack and Coffee*. Boston: Smith & Co., 1887.

Bloodgood, Rev. J.D. *Personal Reminiscences of the War*. New York: Hunt & Easton, 1893.

Booth, John Wilkes. *Right or Wrong, God Judge Me, The Writings of John Wilkes Booth*. Edited by John Rhodehamel and Louise Taper. University of Illinois Press: 1997.

Brooks, Noah. *Washington in Lincoln's Time*. Chicago: Quadrangle Books, 1971.

Craft, David. *History of the One Hundred and Forty-First Regiment Pennsylvania Volunteers*. Towanda, Pa.: Reporter-Journal Printing Co., 1885.

Crowell, J. *The Young Volunteer*. Paterson: The Call, 1906.

Cuffel, Charles. *Durell's Battery in the Civil War*. Philadelphia: Craig, Finley and Co. 1900.

Davis, J. *The Life of David Bell Birney*. Philadelphia: King & Baird, 1867.

de Peyster, John Watts. *Personal and Military History of Philip Kearny*. Elizabeth: Palmer & Co., 1871.

de Trobriand, P. Régis. *Four Years With the Army of the Potomac*. Boston: Ticknor & Co., 1889.

Drake, James Madison. *Historical Sketches of the Revolutionary and Civil Wars*. New York: Webster Press, 1908.

Fletcher, D.C. *Reminiscences of California and the Civil War*. Ayer, Massachusetts: Turner Press, 1894.

Floyd, Fred. *History of the Mozart Regiment*. Boston: Gilston Co., 1909.

Ford, H.E. *History of the 101st N.Y. Regiment*. Syracuse: 1898.

Goss, Warren Lee. *Recollections of a Private*. New York: Crowell & Co. 1890.

Gould, E. K. *Major General Hiram G. Berry*. Rockland, Maine: Press of the Courier-Gazette, 1899.

Hays, Gilbert. *Under the Red Patch*. Pittsburgh: 1908.

Houghton, Edwin. *The Campaigns of the Seventeenth Maine*. Portland: Short & Loring, 1866.

Kearny, Thomas. *General Philip Kearny, Battle Soldier of Five Wars*. New York: Putnam, 1937.

Kiefer Harry M. *Recollections of a Drummer Boy*. New York: Houghton Mifflin Co., 1881.

Kunhardt, Dorothy Meserve and Philip B. Kunhardt Jr. *Twenty Days*. New York: Castle Books, 1965.

Lewis, George. *The History of Battery E, First Regiment Rhode Island Light Artillery*. Providence: Snow & Farnham, 1892.

Long, E.B. *The Civil War Day By Day*. New York: Doubleday, 1971.

Marks, Rev. J. *The Peninsula Campaign in Virginia*. Philadelphia: Lippincott, 1864.

Martin, J.M. *History of the 57th Pennsylvania Veteran Volunteers*. Meadville, Pa.: McCoy & Calvin, n.d.

Pfanz, Harry. *Gettysburg The Second Day*. Chapel Hill: University of North Carolina Press, 1987.

Randall, Ruth. *Lincoln's Sons*. Boston: Little, Brown, & Co., 1955.

Rauscher, Frank. *Music on the March*. Philadelphia: Fell & Co., 1892.

Ray, Frederic. *Alfred Waud, Civil War Artist*. New York: Viking Press, 1974.

Robertson, James I. *Tenting Tonight*. Time-Life Books, 1984.

Rusling, J.F. *Men and Things I Saw in Civil War Days*. New York: Easton & Mains, 1899.

Scott, K. *History of the 105th Pennsylvania Infantry*. Philadelphia: New-World Publishing Co., 1877.

Sears, Stephen. *For Country, Cause, and Leader: The Journal of Charles B. Hayden*. New York: Ticknor & Fields, 1993.

Shreve, William. *The Story of the Third Army Corps Union*. Boston: Hooper Printing Co., 1910.

Swanberg, W.A. *Sickles the Incredible*. New York: Charles Scribner's Sons, 1956.

Tremain, Henry E. *Two Days of War: A Gettysburg Narrative and Other Experiences*. New York: Bonnell, Silver & Bowers, 1905.

Warner, Ezra J. *Generals in Blue*. Baton Rouge: Louisiana State University Press, 1964.

Weygant, Charles. *History of the 124th New York Infantry*. Newburgh: Journal Printing House, 1877.

Newspapers, Magazines & Pamphlets

The Century
Civil War Times Illustrated
Evening Star
Gen. Phil Kearny's Little Bugler
Grand Army Scout and Soldier's Mail
Harper's Weekly
National Intelligencer
National Tribune
New York Herald
New York Sun
New York Sunday Mercury
New York Times
New York Tribune
Philadelphia Inquirer
The Third Army Corps Badge

Special Collections

Gen. David Bell Birney Papers, U.S.A.M.H.I., Carlisle Barracks.
Gen. Philip Kearny Papers, N.J. Historical Society.
Abraham Lincoln Papers, Library of Congress.
Gen. Daniel Sickles Papers, N.Y. Historical Society.

About the Author

William B. Styple is a graduate of Catawba College, and operates a business in his native Kearny, New Jersey, where he is also Town Historian. He has edited and co-authored several works on the Civil War, including the acclaimed *Echoes of the Blue & Gray* video series. He is currently writing the biography of General Philip Kearny.

Other Titles available through Belle Grove Publishing Company:

BOOKS

What Death More Glorious, A Biography of General Strong Vincent.
ISBN 1883926-09-2

Our Noble Blood, The Civil War Letters of General Regis de Trobriand.
ISBN 1883926-10-6

His Proper Post, A Biography of Joshua Lawrence Chamberlain.
ISBN 1-883926-07-6

Andersonville, Giving Up the Ghost.
ISBN 1-883926068

History of the 57th Pennsylvania Infantry.
ISBN 1883926-01-7

Four Years in the Army of the Potomac.
ISBN 1-883926-02-5

With a Flash of His Sword, The Writings of H.S. Melcher, 20th Maine Inf.
ISBN 1883926009

VIDEOS

Echoes of the Blue & Gray, Civil War Veterans on Videocassette,
Volumes I, II & III.

The Splendid Little War.

Gettysburg 1938, The Last Reunion of the Blue & Gray.

AUDIOBOOKS

"Co. Aytch" Memoirs of Sam Watkins, 1st Tennessee Infantry.